THE COMPLETE GUIDE TO
OUTPLACEMENT COUNSELING

THE COMPLETE GUIDE TO OUTPLACEMENT COUNSELING

ALAN J. PICKMAN, PhD
Chemical Bank, New York

Routledge
Taylor & Francis Group
www.routledgementalhealth.com

First Published by Lawrence Erlbaum Associates, Inc., Publishers
10 Industrial Avenue
Mahwah, New Jersey 07430

Transferred to digital printing 2010 by Routledge

Routledge
Taylor and Francis Group
270 Madison Avenue
New York, NY 10016

Routledge
Taylor and Francis Group
2 Park Square
Milton Park, Abingdon
Oxon OX14 4RN

The views expressed in this volume do not necessarily
reflect those of Chemical Bank or its management.

Lawrence Erlbaum Associates, Inc., Publishers
365 Broadway
Hillsdale, New Jersey 07642

Cover design executed by Mairav Salomon-Dekel

Library of Congress Cataloging-in-Publication Data

Pickman, Alan J.
    The complete guide to outplacement counseling / Alan J. Pickman.
        p. cm.

    Includes bibliographical references (p.   ) and index.
    ISBN 0-8058-1647-X. -- ISBN 0-8058-1648-8 (pbk.)
    1. Outplacement services. 2. Vocational guidance. 3. Counselor and client. I. Title.
    HF5381.P52 1995
    331. 12′8068--dc20
                                94-15082
                                CIP

Books published by Lawrence Erlbaum Associates are printed on
acid-free paper, and their bindings are chosen for strength and dura-
bility.

10 9 8 7 6 5 4 3 2

To the memory of my mother, *Berniece Pickman*, and to my father *Simme*—with love and gratitude

Contents

Preface

Outplacement counseling is an important and growing professional service industry in the United States and abroad. In general terms, outplacement counseling is a process of assisting employees who have lost their jobs to develop effective career plans and to find new employment. The need for outplacement services has grown dramatically in the past 15 years, as major U.S. corporations in a wide range of industries have eliminated jobs at the rate of approximately 400,000 per year.

Outplacement counseling has come to be recognized by business managers as a useful and practical tool to assist them in responding to a set of difficult business challenges. With the rapid expansion of the field has come the need to assemble, organize, and clarify the body of knowledge and information that is now available about outplacement. This book is designed as the first one in the field to present authoritative, up-to-date information on a comprehensive range of outplacement topics.

This volume is of value to all those interested in the field including current practitioners, "would-be" practitioners, and human resources professionals. It is also of interest to candidates receiving outplacement services, counseling students, and researchers interested in counseling in business and industry. With such a broad audience in mind it contains a wide range of information. There is both counseling theory and practical suggestions designed especially to assist the practitioner. In addition, there is broad descriptive information around a range of topics that are of value to all readers looking to become more familiar with the field. The book also contains many brief case histories of actual outplacement candidates. Written in nontechnical language, these descriptions bring to life the flavor of outplacement practice.

Work is a central and vital part of adult life. It has always been complicated to assist individuals in making sound career-related decisions. It is more complicated than ever given the rapid social and technological changes taking place throughout the global economy. Millions of individuals have already lost their jobs as a result of these changes. More will, undoubtedly, follow. During the past 20 years the outplacement industry has come to play a significant role in assisting individuals in securing employment and in helping organizations respond to their changing human resources challenges. As a result of its importance, the field of outplacement deserves to be more fully understood, judiciously improved, expertly delivered and wisely used. This book is presented to assist in these efforts.

Overview of Contents

Chapter 1 provides an overview of the field including its history. It also discusses the way in which outplacement services can be provided by both external firms and internal corporate departments. Chapter 2 discusses how outplacement practitioners consult to sponsoring corporate organizations around a full range of job termination issues.

Chapters 3 and 4 discuss how practitioners establish and build effective counseling relationships with individual candidates and the ways in which vocational assessment can be useful. Chapter 5 describes some of the most common barriers to successful job search activities, as well as counselor interventions designed to address and overcome them. Chapter 6 focuses on group outplacement services, whereas chapter 7 examines the distinctive nature of "live-in" outplacement settings and how they can be used to further counseling progress.

Chapters 8 through 10 examine the theoretical foundations of outplacement counseling, as well as certain common patterns of counselor–client interaction. Emphasis is placed on deepening the reader's understanding of the dynamic challenges that this specialized form of counseling presents. Chapters 11 through 13 focus on issues of counselor qualifications and professional development with particular attention on the importance of counselor supervision.

Chapters 14 through 18 examine some special topics in the field including cross-cultural issues, the role of women in outplacement, family issues around job loss, international outplacement activities, and ethics.

Chapter 19 reviews the relation of outplacement counseling to other professional career development activities, and chapter 20 discusses the marketing of outplacement services. Chapter 21 concludes by taking a look at the future of outplacement counseling.

Acknowledgments

The writing of this volume has truly been a collaborative venture. I have received wonderful support, encouragement, and assistance from many people in the outplacement community. If space permitted, I would thank each and every one by name. Even though it is impossible to do so, I must at least acknowledge the following individuals.

First, my thanks to Tish Chamberlain who gave me, as well as scores of others, my first professional opportunity to counsel adults about career issues. Many years later, she provided me with the oppportunity to teach a course on outplacement counseling at New York University's Center for Career and Life Planning. The course preparation enabled me to organize my thoughts about the field. David Rottman convinced me that the course preparation could be converted easily to a full-length book. For this vision, as well as his constant encouragement, progressive management approach, and insightful comments about the text, I am forever grateful. Peter Prichard contributed his thorough knowledge of the field, along with his enthusiasm and generosity of spirit in a way that consistently motivated me.

Many of my other outplacement colleagues provided background information, reviewed chapters, and made excellent suggestons on improving the text. Sheryl Spanier, Jaye Smith, Amy Friedman, and Mary Ann Lee were very helpful in this regard. So were Steve Harrison, Christy Brown, John O'Day, and Faye Woocher. Bob Lee and Jim Gallagher provided me with a perspective on the history of outplacement and helped me to think more clearly about its future. Sandy Bowers taught me many of my early lessons about outplacement practice and has become a stimulating collaborator in more recent years. Barbra Locker, my valued colleague and friend, emboldened me in some of my early efforts at writing about outplacement, and has been a source of support throughout my career.

Thanks must also go to the many outplacement candidates with whom I have worked over the years. Their willingness and ability to share their experiences has enabled me to continue learning about this work. They have all been my teachers. The staff of counselors at Chemical Bank's Career Services Department has also contributed in a major way to this book. They are a highly professional and enormously talented group who both challenge and encourage me. Kelly Johnson assisted with a thorough review of the relevant literature on outplacement. Harriet Greisser shared freely her knowledge of excellent information resources, especially computer-based ones, for outplacement practitioners. My thanks are extended to the professionals at LEA who assisted me with all phases of this project—Amy Pierce, Sharon Levy, Robin Weisberg, and Ray O'Connell. Thanks also to Perre de Clue Scott, Mike Thomas, and Willie Seward for their efficient and responsive administrative support.

It gives me great pleasure to thank Jan Gura, whose loving friendship, enthusiastic support, and creative energy lifted me throughout the writing of this book. Finally, I acknowledge my daughter Sarah Pickman, whose growing curiosity, burgeoning intelligence, and lovable disposition inspire me every day.

—*Alan J. Pickman*

Chapter 1

Introduction

Corporate-sponsored outplacement counseling is an important and growing professional service industry in the United States and in a number of foreign countries. Annual revenues for the outplacement industry grew from approximately $50 million in 1980 to approximately $750 million in 1993. By 1991, 90% of the largest 50 companies in the United States provided some type of outplacement consulting services to their employees who have been affected by downsizings. There are at least 300 outplacement firms in the United States. These organizations employ at least 5,000 individuals, and counsel approximately 1.4 million individuals per year (D.A. Lord, personal communication, December 6, 1993).

What is outplacement counseling? Basically, outplacement counseling is a process of helping employees who have been terminated or whose jobs have been eliminated, to face their job loss with renewed self-confidence, to learn effective job search strategies and techniques, and to conduct a successful job search campaign.

The most comprehensive outplacement programs cover a full range of career-related issues. They begin by counseling the individual client or candidate on how to deal with the emotional issues related to termination. They provide career assessment and assist the client in developing written job search materials including resume, cover letters, and other marketing materials. They then provide interview skills training, assist in the formulation of effective marketing strategies, and review the "dos" and "don'ts" of various job search techniques including networking and responding to newspaper advertisements. Clients are also coached about utilizing executive search and/or placement agencies, and drafting effective letters to use in direct approaches to target companies. Counselors provide motivational support and encouragement throughout the process. The comprehensive programs also provide office and administrative support services that can greatly facilitate the conduct of an effective job search campaign.

History

The origins of outplacement counseling are a bit unclear. Many of the professionals in the field maintain that outplacement began in the United States in the early 1960s when Humble Oil sought assistance for some of its terminated executives. Sol Gruner is generally given credit for designing the services offered in this effort. Some authors, however, trace the beginning of outplacement to Thomas Hubbard of the management consulting firm THINC. Credit is also given to the techniques designed by Bernard Haldane of Haldane Associates in the late 1940s in providing resume, interview skills, and job search training to recently discharged servicemen who were re-entering the civilian job market (Brittain, 1982). Since the early 1960s the outplacement industry has grown to a $750 million business (D.A. Lord, personal communication, July 12, 1993). Growth was slow in the 1960s when the services were offered primarily to the highest level executives. Growth accelerated in the mid- to late-1970s as outplacement was offered more commonly to middle management, technical professionals, and nonofficials.

The growth of outplacement services has evolved in response to the changing employment environment. A number of factors spurred its growth. They included changes in the economy, changes in social conditions, legislative and judicial influences, and shifts in corporate responsibility.

In the late-1970s and 1980s depressed stock values made the acquisition of other companies an attractive corporate strategy for growth. In 1986 alone, there were more than 3,200 mergers and acquisitions. These mergers and acquisitions resulted in job eliminations, downsizings, and management reorganizations. In order to lower costs in the face of stiffer competition, companies streamlined to make their operations more efficient and profitable. "Lean and mean" became the dominant rallying cry of management. Trimming personnel was viewed as the easiest, quickest way to cut costs in the short run. It is estimated that 2.2 million jobs in large corporations disappeared between 1980 and 1985 (Consult America [CA], 1989). An additional 2.3 million jobs disappeared from large U.S. corporations between 1986 and 1992 ("Industry Overviews," 1993).

There were changes in social conditions as well. Providing a work environment that enabled employees to remain with the same company for their entire career was no longer a major corporate objective. Loyalty to employees was weakened in the face of demands for short-term profits and corporate survival. Employees, in turn, felt less bound and committed to their employers.

On the legal front, important legislation enacted during the 1970s and 1980s mandated social changes that affected employment practices. Laws designed to eliminate discrimination in terminations were passed. Also, corporations were looking to protect themselves against lawsuits initiated by discharged employees for wrongful terminations. For these reasons, outplacement came to be seen as an effective human resources management tool.

Finally, there were issues of corporate responsibility. As demands by shareholders for short-term earnings and profits grew, many senior managers chose to reduce the size of the work force in order to have a rapid effect on the bottom line. At the same time, human resources professionals recognized the importance of having their company seen as fair in its employee policies. Having a former employee badmouth a company following termination was not good business practice. It did not promote good community relations, nor foster good morale in the remaining employees. Providing outplacement services came to be seen as very important in maintaining a favorable corporate image. So, all these conditions combined to contribute to the growth of outplacement services. Outplacement counselors became increasingly accepted as facilitators of corporate change.

Professional Associations/Activities

There are two major professional associations in the outplacement field. The Association of Outplacement Consulting Firms (AOCF) is an industry association that represents member outplacement firms. The International Association of Outplacement Professionals (IAOP) represents the individual outplacement practitioners.

Although the birth of corporate-sponsored outplacement took place in the early 1960s, the first professional association in the field, the AOCF, was not formed until May 16, 1982. Its goals are "to deliver quality service in an ethical manner to organizations who sponsor individuals; to produce meaningful research resulting in data that encourages outplacement as an intelligent response to the anguish of termination; to provide a public relations service and to provide a buffer against the attempts by governments to tax, license and regulate" (Le Hane, 1990, p. 41).

The AOCF has grown significantly over the years. It has approximately 65 member firms including seven of the eight largest U.S. firms. Its members represent approximately 65% of the outplacement industry revenues. There are members from around the world including firms in Europe, Asia, South America, and Australia. The use of outplacement firms is growing dramatically in certain of these areas, especially Europe. AOCF members include large, medium, and small firms whose business strategies vary considerably.

In addition to the annual membership meeting, since 1988 the AOCF has also sponsored a yearly professional conference. Attendance has been as high as 350 to 400 people. The conferences include seminars, workshops, keynote addresses, and awards of excellence to corporate organizations that have distinguished themselves in their use of outplacement firms.

A major issue for AOCF in the past few years has been the possible taxation of outplacement services by the federal government. The organization undertook a major lobbying effort to demonstrate that outplacement is a "restorative" and, therefore, nontaxable benefit to the individual, rather than an "augmentative" benefit that would make it taxable. These efforts were made because some government officials viewed outplacement as a perquisite offered only to senior executives that included luxury features such as club memberships, rather than as a service that has been offered to increasingly large numbers of middle managers and nonofficials and that does not include such luxury features. In August 1992 the IRS ruled that the value of corporate-sponsored outplacement services will not be treated as taxable gross income (Harrison, 1992). The industry breathed a collective sigh of relief, as a ruling in the opposite direction would have dealt a stunning blow to the outplacement industry as it currently practices. The AOCF has been active in three other countries—Canada, the United Kingdom, and France—where the tax issue has also emerged. In all cases, the authorities have decided not to consider corporate sponsored outplacement as a taxable benefit.

AOCF represents outplacement firms and their owners. Individual outplacement practitioners did not feel that their specific interests and concerns were being fully addressed by AOCF. So, in 1989 with the active support and backing of AOCF, the IAOP was formed. Its purpose is "to serve, support, develop and unite individual outplacement practitioners." Its mission is to build the professionalism of its members and to achieve recognition of that professionalism. IAOP is designed to serve any individual whose work-related responsibilities or interests are in the area of outplacement without reference to the practitioner's setting. It includes individuals who deliver directly outplacement services to individuals or groups, those who consult directly with the outplaced candidates or corporate sponsors, and those who market outplacement services to client companies. There are also different categories of membership for those individuals whose responsibilities do not include direct delivery of counseling, consulting, or marketing of outplacement services, but whose personal or professional interests are in outplacement or outplacement-related services.

The IAOP was designed to be a grassroots organization that would consist of local chapters. The growth of the organization has been impressive. As of spring 1992 there were more than 800 members. There are 17 regions, 11 in the United States and 6 international, including chapters in the Caribbean, Latin and South America, Asia, Australia, and Europe. A number of standing committees have been charged with establishing guidelines around such topics as ethics, counselor competencies, and program development.

Thus far, the two professional groups, AOCF and IAOP, have cooperated in promoting the growth and advancement of outplacement counseling. However, it is possible that as time goes by their respective interests and agendas, while still overlapping, will diverge in some respects. For example, in spring 1993 the IAOP sponsored its first annual outplacement conference that was held separately from the yearly AOCF gathering.

In summary, these two professional associations encompass a significant percentage of those firms and individuals who are active in the outplacement industry. The growth and development of these associations, especially that of IAOP in the past 4 years, reflect this new industry's ongoing efforts to define both its present and its future.

Internal Versus External Outplacement Services

Outplacement services can be provided by internal programs, external firms of some combination of the two. This section discusses the advantages and disadvantages of the various approaches.

Having terminated an employee, managers might have little desire to have further face-to-face contact with the employee. To do so could be further reminder of a difficult situation. This is one of the main reasons that many managers are very glad to use external outplacement services. They can get help in carrying out a difficult task, and they can then rest easier knowing that the terminated employee is both out of sight and in good hands.

There are other reasons for calling upon external outplacement professionals. Many managers believe that outplacement firms possess greater expertise and sophistication in helping terminated employees. External firms have a staff of counselors dedicated to providing such services. In addition, individual candidates might feel much more free to communicate confidential information to an outsider than they would to an employee of their former organization. Along similar lines, sensitive situations that involve highly personal information might be better handled by outside professional counselors. Furthermore, outplacement firms might be equipped with more comprehensive office support services to assist candidates in conducting a job search campaign.

Not all corporations, however, turn exclusively to external firms for their outplacement needs. There are several models for providing outplacement services internally.

The first model is a program of full-time specialists who perform the full range of outplacement services. They consult with managers in planning and executing downsizings, provide services that might include individual counseling, group workshops, and special offerings. In this model the in-house unit also provides office and administrative support services to assist the candidates in conducting a job search campaign. To justify financially the operation of such a service on an on-going basis, a company must have downsizing efforts underway on a consistent basis. Chemical Bank and Citicorp are two very well-developed examples of this model. Not coincidentally, both are in an industry that experienced major restructuring throughout the 1980s and into the 1990s.

A second model followed by some companies is to provide internal outplacement services on a project basis. In these situations a corporation might establish an internal career center in response to a major downsizing. Employees are then sent to the center where they receive counseling services and office support. The nature of the counseling services that are provided, and the extent of the office support, can vary widely. In some cases it is quite comprehensive; in other cases far more limited. Typically, when the downsizing project ends, the center is shut down as well. In effect, the last person out "shuts off the lights" and the company is no longer in the practice of providing outplacement services.

External firms are very often used even by those companies that provide substantial internal outplacement services. The expertise of the external firms is tapped in a couple of different ways. First, the external firm can consult with the corporate sponsor around establishing an internal career center. The consultation might address issues concerning program design and delivery, communication to employees about the services, and establishment of office support services. In some cases, a representative of the external firm is put in charge of managing the site. In other cases, a representative of the sponsoring company manages the center with or without consultation assistance from the external firm.

A second way in which external firms combine with internal outplacement services is around the assistance provided to senior managers. Senior managers are very often referred to external firms even when high quality internal services are in place. There are at least a couple of explanations for this pattern.

First, the external firms are typically in a position to offer more extensive administrative support services. Most external firms have very well-appointed offices. Options for private offices, dedicated secretarial and administrative assistance, and other amenities exist in the external firms. Senior executives are accustomed to such arrangements. Continued access to such services in the external firms helps soften the psychological blow of termination, as well as facilitating the effective conduct of a job search campaign. In addition, most companies think it important to maintain the special consideration typically afforded to senior executives. To ask them to use the same internal services available to lower level managers or nonofficials, although more democratic, is to negate their senior status in a way that companies choose not to do.

There are several other reasons that a company might choose to provide outplacement services internally rather than using external services. First, it can be cost effective. External outplacement firms typically charge 12%–20% of an executive's compensation for full-service individual outplacement. This can result in very substantial fees, especially when large numbers of high-salaried executives are involved. Some companies think that the job can be done more cheaply internally, and, thereby, it can be offered to more employees. Another potential advantage is that the outplacement services can be integrated more easily and more fully with other human resources services. Also, the visibility of an internal program can serve as concrete proof of the company's commitment to assist those whose jobs have been eliminated. If the center is fortunate enough to receive good word-of-mouth reviews by its clients, this can encourage fuller utilization by those whose jobs are eliminated at a later date.

Having an internal outplacement program is not without its complications. There are several factors that must be considered. The first concerns possible conflicts of interest. Probably the single most important issue in establishing an internal program is credibility. Employees will ask how it is that, on the one hand, a company will eliminate their jobs, but, on the other hand, offer them assistance through an outplacement program. It is critical that the termination decision and the counseling process be seen as separate. Unless this is done, the counselor is put in an awkward position in relation to the candidate, and is unlikely to develop the trust and rapport necessary for a successful counseling relationship. The solution, as practiced by the most successful internal programs, is to build confidence among employees in the outplacement program. This is done most convincingly by demonstrating to the clients that the outplacement counselor is squarely in their corner, and that the counselor was in no way responsible for the decision to terminate.

A second major and related issue is confidentiality. Employees must be assured that no specific revealing information about the content of their counseling sessions will be disclosed to management. The counselor should inform the candidate about the type of information that will be transmitted to management. Usually it is information of a general nature such as start date of counseling, overall progress in search, and, possibly, the type and location of re-employment.

A third issue for internal services is the resistance of executives to use it. Some executives, especially more senior ones, might consider it awkward to be counseled in-house by individuals who previously were subordinate to them. Also, they might be less willing to disclose relevant personal information for fear of exposure.

A final factor that seems to cut both ways is related to re-employment options. For some individuals participating in an internal program perpetuates the notion that they are still part of the organization. This can lead them to think that they have not really been separated, and it can retard their progress in moving forward. This is especially so if they learn of others who have been re-employed in the same company, thus reinforcing the notion that they too will be saved. For others, being a part of an internal program does not lead to the false hope of being saved. It can, however, facilitate their initial networking efforts as they still have ready access to many former colleagues.

In summary, outplacement services can be provided by internal programs, external firms or some combination of both. Management needs to decide which approaches are best suited for their specific circumstances.

Chapter 2

Consulting to Organizations

This chapter focuses on consulting to corporations about outplacement. It includes an examination of issues that affect both the corporate sponsor as well as the individual outplacement candidates. It begins with a discussion of the goals and objectives that a company typically has in utilizing outplacement services.

Reasons for Using Outplacement

There are several reasons for using outplacement services. A major one is to reduce personnel costs in connection with mergers, acquisitions, and downsizings.

The mergers and acquisitions of the 1980s resulted in the joining of organizations each of whom had personnel dedicated to similar functions. In order to make themselves more efficient and profitable, companies looked to eliminate redundancies and overlaps. Trimming personnel was viewed as the quickest way to cut costs in the short run. Outplacement was seen as a way to assist in this process.

Outplacement services have also been used extensively in companies not affected by mergers and acquisitions. A declining economy such as that of the late 1980s and early 1990s brought pressures for employees to be more productive. Restructuring or downsizing were often seen as necessary management responses. Nonproducers were brought more to the attention of managers under such conditions. Although in more profitable times such individuals could be retained despite their limitations, in more difficult times they became more vulnerable. Companies determined that the financial cost of keeping such people on, year after year, far exceeded the cost of providing outplacement services and a one-time offer of severance benefits.

Another consideration for organizations in using outplacement services has to do with public relations. Companies are mindful about their public images. It is important for them to be seen as showing care and concern for job eliminees, rather than merely dumping them without regard. Word about the way in which a company handles terminations spreads quickly throughout industry networks, especially if they are handled clumsily. The reputation a company develops can have a bearing on its ability to attract and retain desirable employees. So, employing outplacement services can help maintain or create a positive public image.

Another reason for using outplacement services is to maintain in-house morale. No matter how well a termination is handled, fear and anxiety can spread throughout the organization. Employees wonder whether they will be next. In the face of such anxiety, motivation can wane and productivity can decrease. Morale can be jeopardized unless the situation is addressed and handled by management. Knowing that outplacement services are being offered to the job eliminees can have a positive affect on the survivors. Although it might not completely calm employees' fears, it does provide reassurance to know that if they are to be next, they can expect the same assistance that was offered to their former colleagues.

Outplacement services are also seen as a way to avoid costly litigation. Job eliminees might feel angry and resentful and conclude that they were discriminated against around issues of age, race, or gender. Litigation is time consuming and expensive for all the involved parties. If an individual is engaged in an outplacement process and being assisted in moving forward in a productive, creative way, it reduces the likelihood of lawsuits. As some in the outplacement industry are fond of saying, "People who are speaking to outplacement counselors are not speaking to attorneys about how they were mistreated" (Sweet, 1989, p. 160).

Finally, sometimes outplacement services are used to ease out an employee for political or stylistic reasons. Surveys have shown that in as many as 75% of the cases, executives are fired for reasons other than poor performance. They are let go because of relationship problems or stylistic differences, most often with their boss (Sweet, 1989). Outplacement services are used to facilitate such changes.

Consulting With Managers for Use of Outplacement Counseling

How Do Outplacement Counselors Assist Managers?

The growth of corporate-sponsored outplacement certainly suggests that corporations view it as a valuable service. One reason for its popularity is that it assists managers in a difficult task. Terminating employees is consistently ranked by managers as one of the most difficult and distasteful of their responsibilities. So, for many managers, being able to call upon experts to assist them in this process is very welcome.

Inexperienced managers might need help in all aspects of the termination process. Among the issues to be attended to are choosing the appropriate person to do the terminating and designating the best time for the interview; preparation of a statement of severance benefits and other necessary documentation; conducting the termination interview in a manner that is clear, direct and compassionate.

Terminating an employee can be difficult even for more experienced managers. Even tough managers might find themselves stammering and struggling. They might have feelings of empathy for the terminated employee who could be a co-worker or colleague of long standing. Some managers might feel personally guilty about inflicting discomfort or pain on others even though they recognize they are acting as agents for a more impersonal entity, the company, and that their action is necessary on behalf of the company.

Kate A.[1] was an experienced human resource manager who was forced to eliminate the job of one of her direct reports, an individual with whom she had worked for the past 3 years. Although Kate had coached many others over the years about conducting termination interviews, the situation was clearly different for her when it hit so close to home. In anticipation of the meeting she asked to be coached on issues about which she had considerable direct experience. What should she say? How will she keep it brief? What will she do if her supervisee gets emotional? How can she deliver the news and still hope to maintain a positive relationship in the future? We reviewed her concerns, discussed some specific interventions and acknowledged together how much more complicated it can be to carry out professional responsibilities when it involves a close associate or friend.

Outplacement counselors can enter a job elimination or termination situation at a variety of different points in the process. Their entry is often determined by the prior experience and degree of comfort of the company managers in carrying out such actions. If called upon for an early intervention, outplacement counselors will work with the company manager to see to it that the ending is handled effectively and professionally. This requires attention to five major areas: documentation, communication, legal considerations, termination interview, and administrative.

Documentation.   Information must be gathered to define, verify, and record all necessary information about an ending. A company needs to have or develop a standard review and approval process before an individual is terminated.

Communication.   Decisions need to be made about what is going to be said and to whom about a termination. This can include internal communications, external communications, and the direct communication to those being terminated.

Legal Considerations.   This concerns the legal obligations of the relationship between organization and individual. Among the issues to be considered are the terms of termination, contractual obligations (real or imagined) and Equal Employment Opportunity (EEO) implications. Once again, it is important for companies to have policies or procedural guidelines around these issues.

---

[1]All names used in referring to specific candidates are fictitious in order to preserve confidentiality.

Termination Interview.   Among the issues to be considered are who will be present at the interview, when will the interview be held, and where will the interview be held. Careful consideration must be given to the termination message itself. A factual, objective, concise message must be delivered, and possible employee reactions must be anticipated. Preparation is a key. In general, the most emotionally charged aspect of a termination for managers is the termination interview.

Like many managers with little experience in this area, Rene asked for guidance about what he should say when called upon to do his first termination interview. We agreed that his remarks should be clear, direct, and succinct, but, at the same time, be expressed in a compassionate, humane, and respectful fashion. We agreed on the following as his introduction:

> John, I've requested our meeting to inform you about an important decision that has been made. As a result of our recent merger with Acme Co., a downsizing will be taking place. After a careful review, we've concluded that we will have to cut back a large number of positions, and yours is one of the jobs that is being eliminated. I can assure you that the decision was not made lightly. The situation was reviewed by the entire management team.

> We can appreciate that this might be difficult for you. I would like to use part of today's meeting to inform you about the services which we will be providing to assist you in moving forward. We have engaged the services of a well-regarded outplacement firm, D.D.&S., which, if you wish, will be available for your use. Specifically, we also want to inform you about some of the details and procedures that are involved in making this transition. We have prepared a letter outlining the arrangements, and I would like to review it with you.

Administrative.   This refers to the preparation of a termination letter. It is sound management practice to prepare a termination letter. It provides the terminated individual with a written confirmation of the termination discussion and it covers the administrative bases. This is important because the emotional nature of the conversation can result in the individual not recalling accurately many details. In addition to providing a written summary of what was said, it reinforces in writing that the termination is real and irrevocable. This can help to reduce any disbelief that the individual harbors about what has taken place.

The tone of the letter should be businesslike and professional. The items to be included will vary depending on such factors as the level of the individual being terminated and the circumstances around the termination (e.g., layoff vs. performance). Among the items to be addressed are the confirmation of an effective date of termination, the amount and payment format (e.g., lump sum vs. bridging) of the severance, and the amount, if any, of vacation pay.

The termination letter should be signed by a responsible authority in the organization and the terminated employee. Some organizations ask that the document be notarized for the protection of both signatories.

As indicated earlier, outplacement counselors can be called upon to consult with company managers around just a few aspects of the termination process or around all aspects. Typically, the less experienced the managers, the more consultation is requested.

In summary, outplacement counselors assist client organizations in planning and executing terminations so that they are conducted in a professional and humane fashion. Terminating an employee is one of the most difficult and undesirable responsibilities of a manager. Outplacement counselors can consult with managers about a full range of issues so that the terminations are handled with skill, flexibility, and sound judgment.

Chapter 3

Establishing the Counseling Relationship

Most outplacement firms will recommend that individual clients be introduced to their outplacement counselors as soon as possible after the termination. This chapter examines how the counseling relationship is established.

The first task for the outplacement counselor is to begin building trust and rapport with the client. The trust provides a foundation for the counseling relationship. The way in which the trust is established will vary from one situation to the next depending on the circumstances.

For example, in certain situations the individual is not at all unhappy about the job elimination. John was a 29-year-old bright, skillful, highly presentable individual with a specialty in corporate finance. He was financially responsible only for himself. He had been in the same position for the 5 years since graduating with an MBA from a well-regarded institution. Although he continued to receive excellent performance evaluations, he had become restless in the job during the past 12 months. He viewed the job elimination as an opportunity to make a change, and was excited at the possibility of being assisted in his career planning by an outplacement firm with an excellent reputation. He had never previously received any professional career planning assistance. John and his counselor hit the ground running. Their first session was characterized by a lively exchange of information and a high degree of trust and rapport.

On the other hand, George was a 50-year-old individual who had been in the real estate and facilities management area for the past 25 years. He had worked for a number of different organizations, never moving beyond lower to middle-level management. Although the stated reason for his referral to outplacement was a job elimination, there was some evidence to suggest that his managers were no longer comfortable with his contribution to the unit. George was remarried and had child support and alimony obligations. He had access to a company car, but was required to return it on the day he was informed about the job elimination. In his initial meeting with the outplacement counselor, George appeared angry and tense. He reported being surprised at the decision to eliminate his job. He expressed great concern about finding a job in his field given his age and the marketplace conditions in real estate. He reported having little financial back-up beyond the modest severance that was being paid to him. He questioned how outplacement was going to be helpful to him. The first several sessions were characterized by a considerable display of anger and distrust by George. The trust and rapport with his counselor built very slowly for the first half dozen sessions.

Both counselor and client bring a unique combination of skill, style, temperament, and prior experience to the counseling situation. Consequently, each counseling relationship will develop somewhat differently. It is possible, however, to discuss some general patterns and themes.

We have discussed, in an earlier section, what the benefits are to the sponsoring organization of providing outplacement services. At this point it is useful to consider the benefits that candidates expect from outplacement. These expectations affect the level of motivation that candidates bring to outplacement services.

Individuals vary significantly at the outset in terms of how much they understand about outplacement and how helpful they expect it to be. Some come to the initial contact with the outplacement counselor convinced that the services will be helpful. They might have been exposed to a trusted colleague who has already used outplacement services and reported favorably on them. This happens quite frequently in an in-house outplacement unit where the word can travel quickly along the "grapevine" about the nature and quality of services being provided by the employer. Or, they might be well aware that they have not planned or managed their career in the most effective manner, and welcome the assistance of a trained professional.

Others come to the outplacement services expecting very little of a positive nature. Their expectations might be low because they have little information about the services. Some think it is nothing more than resume writing assistance. Others come convinced that because they have changed jobs in the past or hired new employees they know all there is to know about job search.

One of the first tasks of the outplacement counselor is to communicate to clients what services are offered and how they can be of benefit. The benefits fall into three major categories: (a) emotional support and motivation, (b) concrete assistance around career planning and job search, (c) administrative support services.

Emotional Support and Motivation

Clients can experience a wide range of emotions during the outplacement experience. Anger, pain, fear, disappointment, relief, excitement, hopefulness—these are just some of the feelings that can occur during the course of the outplacement services. Consequently, the outplacement counselor can be called upon to provide a substantial amount of emotional support.

Roberta O. experienced a good deal of excitement and hopefulness at the start of outplacement. She was a 48-year-old woman who had only one employer since she entered the work world 25 years ago. She was a lower level officer in a controllership area. At the time her job was eliminated due to a downsizing she was offered another position within the organization. She elected not to take it and opted instead for the severance package. She told her counselor that if she was ever going to leave the nest, now was the time. Should she return to college? Try another industry? Remain in banking? She came to the outplacement offices with a sense of excitement about future possibilities combined, admittedly, with some nervousness about venturing out into unfamiliar territory.

Rachel B. came to outplacement with a very different set of emotions. She felt victimized about the circumstances that brought her to outplacement. She had been with the organization for more than 20 years. When a reorganization reduced her department head count from five to two, she tried to pick up the slack by working longer and longer hours. She did not try to clarify with her managers the implications of this reduction for the long-term viability of the department. The manager, for his part, did not volunteer any clarifying information to her, as an effective manager should.

She continued to work very hard, apparently acting on the assumption that, if she worked in this way, her job would be safe. Unfortunately, it was a bargain she had struck with herself, but not one that her management had agreed to in any way. Consequently, when her job was eliminated several months later, she felt betrayed and used. Although she eventually worked through these feelings with the assistance of her counselor, she began outplacement in a state of anger, disappointment, and fear.

As these examples suggest, clients typically experience a lot of emotion at the beginning of outplacement. The job termination is still fresh. Some individuals, perhaps as many as one third, are able to move into the counseling process and begin their job search without much difficulty. Others, however, experience significant anger, pain, and fear about the future. This is very often true of long-service clients. These are individuals who might have worked for the same employer for their entire career. They typically joined the organization at a time when job security was almost assured in the absence of a gross offense. Suddenly, they find themselves severed from the only organization they have ever known. A major component of their self-concept is shaken badly, as well as their sense of order about the world of work. It is as if the rules of the game have been arbitrarily cast aside and they are disoriented and, seemingly, without resources to cope with an uncertain future.

Hal was a successful 50-year-old operations officer with 21 years of experience at a major financial institution. Hal was tall and trim; he appeared very fit and healthy. His work success was a source of great pride; he was also a visible role model in his community. Loyalty to the company was a guiding principle for him. When Hal first met his counselor a few days after his job elimination, he was a shaken man. His hands trembled, his eyes were swollen from several sleepless nights, he made minimal eye contact. He responded to her questions in monosyllables, he withdrew into a corner of the outplacement center and had minimal contact with other clients. Those who were familiar with him barely recognized him for the first few weeks. Gradually, he began to engage more fully with his outplacement counselor. With her encouragement and support, he began to articulate how disappointed he was about the job elimination, and how concerned he was about disappointing those in his community who looked up to him. In addition, he described how unfair it felt to him that his many years of loyal service did not spare him this perceived indignity. It took close to 6 months for him to hit his full stride in job search, and more than 1 year before he landed a comparable position.

Models for Understanding Loss

As we know from the work of Kubler-Ross (1975), any severe loss results in grief. Losing a job certainly qualifies as a major loss (Holmes & Rahe, 1967) and it can trigger the states of a grieving process as described by Kubler-Ross.

First, candidates can experience shock and disbelief. They are stunned. It is as if their world is coming to an end. The shock can be accompanied by denial. Denial can take the form of withdrawing into a protective shell or pretending not to be disappointed by the job elimination.

Those who withdraw into the shell can take weeks before they are willing and able to begin extroverted job search activity such as networking or other face-to-face contact. If they engage in any search activity at all at the outset, it is of the more passive variety (e.g., letter writing, responding to newspaper ads) all of which can be done from the safety of the outplacement offices.

Other clients maintain that they are neither angry nor disappointed by the termination, despite verbal and nonverbal behavior to the contrary. One client ended our first meeting by informing me "that the walls of your office should not have been painted red because it elicits angry feelings in *other* people"—this despite the fact that the office had been recently painted in a carefully chosen soft pink pastel color designed to create a calming effect. Counselors should take note of behavioral cues from clients such as flattened affect, loss of energy, difficulty in concentration, muscle tension, confusion, tangential speech, and reports of numbness that might suggest the initial shock stage.

A second stage is marked by strong active emotion. Although it might be sadness, it is more likely to be anger. The candidate can feel outrage at having been terminated after years of loyal service. Feelings of powerlessness and helplessness are common, given that the ending was not on the employee's terms.

One rather common manifestation of this anger is the client's attitude toward the bridging pay that many companies provide to assist the individual in making the transition to a next position. A recent survey of 500 major companies conducted by Coopers & Lybrand (1991) demonstrated that approximately 40% of the companies provide severance in the form of bridging pay where an individual is, in effect, kept on the payroll for a pre-determined period, rather than being given a lump sum payment at the time of termination. Outplacement counselors observe that the manner of severance payment can influence client behavior during the search period.

Mike M., a mid-level executive in his 50s with 19 years of service, was an example in saying that "I'm not going to begin my search in earnest until the end of my bridging approaches so that I can get every penny of bridging pay that the company owes me. I want to take as much from them as possible. Why shouldn't I?" Mike's anger and his attitude toward the bridging pay slowed his progress considerably in outplacement. His counselor tried a variety of interventions to facilitate Mike's progress. However, there was little change in his level of job search activity until 2 months before the scheduled end of the bridging pay. At that point the pace of his activity accelerated, and he landed a job within several more months. He was one of the clients who "succeeded" in exacting his full measure of financial revenge at the company.

The third stage is characterized by deepening sadness or grief. This period might also be accompanied by feelings of lowered self-worth. The deepening sadness results from the recognition that something major has been lost and is not to be returned.

According to Bridges (1988) there are a number of different types of loss that the individual can experience in connection with job termination. First, there can be the loss of attachments. Job loss changes an individual's specific relationships, group membership, and feelings of being connected to something larger than himself. Co-workers are gone, as are bosses and subordinates. Also gone is the sense of being part of an organization from which a sense of pride or strength or belonging can be derived.

A second loss is that of turf. This can include the individual's physical territories and/or fields of responsibility. The physical location, size, and characteristics of one's working area are an important aspect of turf. Many of those in outplacement experience this loss as they go from a private office in their former employer to the shared office carrels of the outplacement firm. Also, their former employer had developed a division of labor, so that everyone had a place and a predictable way of participating in the joint effort. So, for example, all questions about computers went to John, all questions about marketing to Mary, and so forth. These fields of responsibility are part of John and Mary's turf. Both the physical space and fields of responsibility are lost with job termination.

Third, there can be a loss of psychological structure. All the patterns of authority, policies, schedules, and deadlines constitute structure for an employee. These structures protect individuals from feeling like their life is unpredictable and chaotic. Those who depend a great deal on externally imposed structure will be most disrupted by the loss of structure following job termination. When confronted by job loss, such individuals are almost like deep-sea divers who depressurize too quickly.

A fourth type of loss that can be experienced following job termination is the loss of a sense of future. Although individuals might not be mindful of it until it is disrupted, most individuals carry around a notion of an expected future in their heads and hearts. Whether it is referred to as a plan or a dream or a vision, it is an idea about what the future will be like. Job loss can be very disturbing if it threatens us to the point of where we think our dreams will not be realized. Individuals vary in terms of how important the future dream is to them, and how easily it can be altered. Some can generate the vision of a revised future quickly, whereas others take a long time to derive a new plan following job loss.

Loss of control is yet another category. Job termination can produce a sense that life is up for grabs and that attempts at influencing outcomes are not likely to be effective. Like with the other types of loss, some people are hit harder by this one than others. Typically, those who like to be in control at all times— days planned to the minute, outcomes expected, results easily measurable—are most at risk for this type of loss.

Grant H. and Alice B. reflect the way in which different individuals are affected differently by loss. Grant is a mid-50s computer and systems expert. He has a doctorate from a highly selective university, 15 years experience as a scientist/researcher at a world-renowned laboratory, followed by 10 years at prestigious financial institutions. Grant was very much at sea about the loss of psychological structure and the loss of control following his job elimination. He asked virtually every counselor at the outplacement setting to provide him with systematic, step-by-step procedures concerning various job search topics, even though he was told repeatedly that there were no such cut-and-dried approaches. He insisted that he be told the most logical way to pursue his job search. His questions reflected a very strong desire to restore a sense of control and structure, both of which were knocked out for him with the job loss. On the other hand, Grant never once mentioned in outplacement his feelings of attachment or connection to any former colleagues, or supervisors, nor did he express any sense of interpersonal loss.

Alice, for her part, was just the opposite. The most painful losses for her were the work-related attachments and affiliations. She was a middle-aged, unmarried woman who had worked in the same department for the past 12 years. She had formed a number of very close relationships with co-workers. They felt like family to her, especially given that her blood relatives were few, and lived in other regions of the country. The disruption of these valued work relationships was the focus of much of her early discussion in outplacement. Alice's progress in job search accelerated as she began to build some new relationships with her peers at the outplacement center.

The recognition of these various types of loss, painful as it might be, paves the way for the acceptance of the job loss as definitive. With acceptance comes the possibility of considering new jobs or options. Self-esteem improves, optimism prevails, and the motivation to plan and conduct a job search campaign is evident.

For some candidates these stages might be so subtle as to be hardly noticeable. They last only a few days. For others they are wrenching and disruptive and can stretch out for months before the candidate is ready to consider alternatives realistically and to act decisively in a search campaign. Still others begin the counseling process energetically and with no apparent difficulty only to hit a slump 6 or 8 weeks later. For these individuals the emotional reactions are delayed, but they still hit hard.

The practical counseling implications of all this is that outplacement practitioners are called upon to deal with a very wide range of emotions. They must be able to determine accurately how much attention must be given to the grieving process and when candidates are ready to move into the planning and campaign phases.

As the search campaign unfolds candidates must be educated about the emotional roller coaster that is likely. Candidates must be supported or confronted in the inevitable "ups and downs," especially if their campaign lasts for many months.

Issues around long-term clients and protracted job searches are complicated and are discussed much more fully in a later chapter. There are a few things to be said now, however, about providing emotional support and motivation during the middle and late stages of job search.

First, the challenge of providing support and motivation in the middle and late stages might be different from that of providing them at the outset. At the outset, the counselor's tasks often revolve around establishing the initial trust and rapport and providing concrete information. Following the initial phases of the search, the counselor's role might shift and the techniques necessary to enact the new roles might need to be different. For example, the counselor's role might shift to that of job campaign manager or coach. This requires the ability to monitor closely the candidate's campaign activities, to identify early problems or hurdles, and to call these to the attention of the candidate as clearly as possible. This set of counselor behaviors is more difficult for some than for others. It can require counselors to confront clients more frequently, while at the same time continuing to build trust and rapport.

Protracted job searches can also affect counselors differently. Some counselors are at their best in the initial phases of counseling, whereas others are temperamentally suited to "go the distance." For example, certain counselors are most interested in the start-up phases of activity when the situation is new and fresh and learning is taking place at a rapid pace. When the newness wears off, some interest and enthusiasm is lost. Others are better suited to sustaining a high level of interest and enthusiasm even when the newness has passed. Counselors must strive to remain helpful and effective even in the face of protracted job searches. This can be very difficult to do, especially when client frustration is high and fresh ideas are hard to identify. More is said, in a later chapter, about some approaches and techniques for managing long-term counseling relationships.

Chapter 4

Assessment in Outplacement Counseling

Assessment is an important part of the outplacement counseling process. This chapter examines some of the topics that are typically addressed in assessment as well as some of the professional issues raised in connection with assessment.

There are two major goals in assessment. The first is to gain as complete a picture as possible of the client. This can include information about values, interests, skills, style, and vocational dreams. It is important to remember that this information is being used so that the clients can understand as much about themselves as possible. This will enable them to make more informed decisions about their jobs, career, and lifestyle.

The second major goal of assessment is to promote enhanced self-esteem in the client. Many candidates find it difficult to articulate those skills that they use in carrying out their work-related responsibilities. They get so accustomed to completing their assigned tasks on a day-to-day basis, that it becomes difficult to analyze accurately what skills are being applied. For example, Bernadette was a clerical worker who said that she "just entered data into the computer, that's all I do." However, following some probing by her counselor, she was able to see that a number of skills were involved in carrying out her job. First, she was attentive to detail. She was accurate. She performed well under difficult conditions. Her work product did not suffer under the pressure of end-of-the month deadlines. She cooperated well with co-workers. She demonstrated helpfulness by explaining procedures to new workers. When Bernadette was helped to see her achievements more clearly, and to understand the skills required to produce the achievements, her self-esteem began to rise. She realized that she was capable of doing more than just "entering data into the computer."

Who Should Be Assessed?

The following guidelines are used by one of the leading national outplacement firms, Lee Hecht Harrison (R. Lee, 1987) to determine whether formal assessment is warranted.

Testing is indicated for:

1. clients who must change career directions because of adverse labor market conditions;
2. clients who were terminated from their previous positions because of difficulties in the areas of management style, interpersonal competence, or personal motivation;
3. clients who are experiencing serious stress due to the manner and/or circumstances of the termination, or the stresses of the job search itself;
4. clients who request testing because they want to use this opportunity to learn as much as possible about themselves; and
5. clients who appear to have long-standing emotional adjustment difficulties if the consultant needs this information in order to make a decision about a possible clinical referral.

Based on these guidelines, it follows that the amount and type of assessment undertaken will vary from client to client. The decision to expose clients to formal assessment techniques should be based on a carefully considered rationale. Counselors should be clear about the goals and objectives of the assessment and see to it that appropriate instruments are chosen. Some of the topics most frequently addressed in assessment are discussed here.

Dreams

Early childhood is the time when individuals begin to have thoughts and dreams about what they would like to be and do in the future. These thoughts can be expressed through fantasies, wishes, play, the arts, and the selection of reading material. In many cases, unfortunately, these dreams are not fulfilled. Realities such as time, money, talent, and motivation intervene and alter the dreams. One of the first and, sometimes, most exciting tasks for outplacement clients is to reconnect via assessment to these early dreams. There are a variety of methods for doing so. Counselors will vary in their approach. The basic task is to help clients rediscover these early dreams and wishes in order to determine whether they can influence future directions.

Counselors are called upon to strike a delicate balance around the topic of dreams. They need to be mindful of both possibilities and limitations. For some clients, counselors need to encourage expansion and to help clients resist prematurely the "yes, buts..." of reality. For other clients, counselors need to interject reality data so that such information can be considered along with the dreams and fantasies.

Doug K. was an example of the former; he needed help in expanding his horizons in connection with career planning. Doug had worked as a mid-level back-office operations officer in the same financial services organization for more than 20 years. He never imagined that his job would be eliminated and had given very little thought to other career possibilities. As his job search dragged on, Doug's counselor assisted him in reconnecting to his early interest in antique glass. With much encouragement from the counselor Doug met a number of local craftsmen and learned much more about this trade. At last report he was apprenticing himself to a local glazier with an eye toward opening his own business. Expanding Doug's vision about future possibilities was a major contribution made by the counselor.

Warren, on the other hand, was assisted greatly by a counselor who focused him on certain reality considerations that eventually tempered his dream. Warren was in his early 30s, recently married, and a graduate of a prestigious business school. He prided himself on his entrepreneurial spirit. At the outset of outplacement counseling, Warren indicated that he thought there was a market for a high-quality child-care facility. He saw this as a potentially lucrative avenue, as well as a way to offer a much needed service. It also coincided with his life stage, as he and his wife anticipated having children in the next several years. After a rather lengthy investigation he concluded, to his dismay, that real estate and labor costs, in combination with numerous regulations made the venture not viable. His counselor assisted Warren most by helping him to identify and evaluate clearly the realistic hurdles and obstacles while not dampening prematurely his enthusiasm for this dream.

Values

Values are ideas that we hold dear. Each of us has a different set of values, attributing more importance to some than to others. For example, some individuals value independence and personal freedom more than security and friendly relationships. Others value high income rather than personal growth.

Different jobs and work environments have different values that are reflected in them. For example, some situations value individual initiative and enterprise; others value adherence to established rules and procedures. The task of counselor and client is to find the best fit between the value requirements of the job and the client's personal value system. This is not always easy to do as the values inherent in a job or organization are not always apparent, nor the weight attached to them easy to discern. Inferences often have to be made in assessment of job–person fit around values.

Bernetta is an example of an individual who found a job in an organization whose guiding values were more consistent with her own. She had worked in the accounting department of a large bank for many years. Although she carried out the technical requirements of her job quite well, she found limited satisfaction in it. She was much more enthusiastic about her church-related involvements, because they provided a sense of contributing to her community. Her job search ended happily when she secured a position doing similar accounting work at her local community hospital. She felt that the values and mission of the organization were a much better fit for her than those of the bank.

Interests

Interests are preferences for particular activities. An identification of both career and noncareer related interests is an important consideration in gaining as complete a picture as possible of clients.

The most widely used interest inventory is the Strong Interest Inventory (SII; Hansen & Campbell, 1985). It compares the interests of the client with those of individuals who already work in approximately 110 different occupations, and who report being satisfied in their work. It also reports scores on 23 basic interest areas and 6 Holland themes based on John Holland's (1973) theory of occupational personalities. The SII rests on the assumption that "birds of a feather, flock together." In other words, the more an individual's interests match those of the people with whom he works, the greater the likelihood of his being satisfied in the work environment. The SII can be particularly helpful in providing a broad overview of the range of occupations that exist, especially for those individuals who do not know a lot about occupations other than their own.

For other clients, the SII provides much needed confirmation about certain themes and/or occupations which they were already considering. For example, Richard R. had held a variety of entrepreneurial positions in a number of different areas including television commercial production, publishing, and copywriting. His most recent position was dissatisfying because of its narrow scope and lack of independence. The SII helped to confirm several points for him. First, he was most interested in those occupations that left room for his creative interests, while at the same time allowed him to operate in an autonomous and entrepreneurial fashion. Second, he had a wide range of interests. He preferred those situations that were multidimensional and where he could be involved in a range of activities. After reviewing the SII results, he left counseling with a much strengthened conviction that the direction he had been actively considering was, indeed, right for him.

Skills/Achievements

Skills or abilities are difficult to measure directly for adults in business occupations, other than in the case of very concrete skills such as the manual dexterity required to complete certain motoric tasks. This is especially true for most of the individuals seen in outplacement whose skills are not of such a concrete nature. Therefore, counselors must rely on a careful analysis of the client's record of achievements in order to identify transferable skills.

There are a number of different instruments for this purpose. Most of them ask the client to produce a list of accomplishments and achievements. The list is reviewed and elaborated upon in discussions with the counselor. The purpose of this discussion is to identify those skills demonstrated in the accomplishments so that the client can begin thinking more clearly how the skills can be transferred to other jobs and settings.

Type/Temperament

Temperament or interpersonal style is a broad category. Assessment in this area can be useful in providing clients data on some of their more dominant tendencies. For example, some individuals prefer working in group activities, whereas others prefer working alone or with one other. The most widely used of the instruments in this category is the Myers–Briggs Type Indicator (MBTI; Myers & McCaulley, 1985). The MBTI is based on Carl Jung's (1971) typology of personalities. The MBTI can command client attention because it allows for the examination of individual differences in a nonjudgmental, nonevaluative way. Although it is not possible to mention the ever-growing body of research literature on the MBTI, suffice it to say that it has been used increasingly in recent years in career counseling and organizational applications. Among the issues to which it has been applied are determining job–person fit and understanding individual differences around supervisory, managerial, and leadership approaches. It helps clients to see how certain types result in different ways of thinking, deciding, and behaving.

Practice Issues in Assessment

At this point some remarks are in order about the way in which tests are used in practice by outplacement counselors, as well as about some of the issues raised by their use.

A first issue concerns the background and training of the tester in outplacement firms. Some firms have psychologists administer the tests. The psychologist can either be a full-time employee, on retainer, or a member of an outside firm. Sometimes the psychologist will only be involved in administering the tests and interpreting the results; other times the psychologist will be the primary or secondary counselor throughout the outplacement process.

Other firms involve all the counselors in assessment. This raises the issue of the extent to which the tester is fully trained and qualified for assessment. Most firms who take this approach limit the testing done by the nonpsychologist consultants. The battery might include an interest inventory such as the Strong Interest Inventory and a style test such as the MBTI, and a skills inventory. In this way, the firm decreases the likelihood that counselors are using assessment tools that exceed their level of competence. However, the issue of training for testing remains a delicate one in outplacement. In many cases, outplacement counselors are administering and interpreting assessment tools despite not having had extensive training in this area. Care must be taken to ensure that counselors understand both the benefits and limitations of assessment tools, as well as their own strengths and limitations as testers.

A second issue concerns the extent of testing and the nature of the feedback. Good judgment must be exercised in selecting those tests to be administered. Although it might be appropriate to provide a more extensive battery to a client who is seriously considering a career change, it might be less appropriate to test as extensively those individuals who state clearly that they are seeking career continuation. Or, alternatively, it might be that career continuation candidates are not given an extensive battery at the outset. Rather, they are assisted in launching a job search quickly at their insistence. Then, if their initial efforts do not produce significant results, they might be more receptive later to more extensive testing and feedback.

As for the interpretation of results, several issues are important. The first is to realize that the tests typically used in outplacement involve self-assessment. The data come from the client's own choices. Counselors, therefore, should not mystify the process or inappropriately suggest that the data reveals hidden parts of the self.

Another issue concerns the presentation of test data in comprehensible fashion. Counselors must present the data in a way that allows clients to absorb it. As counselors present the data and identify patterns, consistencies and discrepancies, they should also check for feedback from the clients to make sure the interpretations are understood. Providing written profiles can be especially useful as it allows clients to review the results again at their leisure.

Another issue is the extent to which the purpose of the assessment is kept clearly in mind. The information about dreams, values, skills, accomplishments, and style is generated so that clients can understand themselves as fully as possible and make more informed decisions about job, career, and lifestyle. The results are generally most helpful when the tester has some rationale for administering them and some specific issues in relation to which the specific test data will be useful. Assessment should not be done merely to satisfy the curiosity of the counselor or because the firm requires that all clients take certain tests.

In summary, assessment is an important part of the outplacement process. Counselors need to establish guidelines that assist them in determining the amount and type of assessment to be undertaken with individual clients. Among the topics that can be addressed via assessment are client skills, achievements, interests, style, values, and vocational dreams. There are also a host of practice issues to be considered in conducting assessment.

Chapter 5

Barriers to Successful Job Search

There is a range of topics that forms the basis of most comprehensive outplacement services. The topics typically include self-assessment and goal setting, resume preparation, interviewing, and salary negotiation. In addition, attention is paid to various job search methods such as networking, direct mail, and advertisements. Further topics include researching the job market and working with executive recruiters.

There are a number of excellent books that address these job search topics in considerable detail. Among them are *What Color is Your Parachute?* (Bolles, 1994), *The Complete Job Search Handbook* (Figler, 1988), and *Through the Brick Wall* (Wendleton, 1992). The reader is encouraged to refer to these books for job search information. Rather than cover the same ground, this volume examines a different dimension of the various job search topics. It focuses on the internal or psychological barriers and blocks that hinder candidates from taking successful job search action around these various topics. In addition, this chapter identifies some of the most frequent rationalizations that clients provide for their difficulties in taking job search action.

The purpose of identifying these barriers or rationalizations is to highlight them more clearly so that they can be addressed earlier and more effectively in the job search process. In some cases, the barriers can be overcome with additional information, but, in many cases, there is a need to address the attitudes and feelings that underlie the barriers. The chapter begins by addressing each job search topic and highlighting some of the major barriers associated with it. It then synthesizes some of the major themes that cut across the various topics and discusses counseling interventions to address these barriers.

Job Search Topics and Their Barriers

Self-Assessment

The first topic is self-assessment. This topic is typically addressed early in the job search process in order to assist candidates in identifying more clearly their interests, skills, accomplishments, style, and vocational dreams. Among the barriers and rationalizations that might restrict candidates around self-assessment are the following:

- Dislike for taking tests. Candidates have had prior experience with assessment and found it too evaluative, limiting, and/or not useful.
- Fear of exposure. Candidates are concerned that the assessment tools will reveal too much personal information about them.
- Waste of valuable time. Candidates are eager to begin full-scale job search activities and see assessment as taking too much time and slowing them down.
- Uninformed about potential benefits of assessment. Some candidates are not familiar with assessment instruments and do not know what they could gain from them.
- Unnecessary. Some candidates believe that they know themselves very well already and have nothing to gain from an assessment process.
- Assessment is too psychologically oriented. Some candidates think assessment is too much like going to a "shrink" and they are, therefore, not interested.

Resume Preparation

A next topic is resume preparation. There are a variety of internal barriers and rationalizations that impede candidates in successfully completing a resume. Among them are:

- Nothing to say. Some candidates feel like they have not accomplished very much and do not have many skills. Therefore, they fear the resume will look thin and unimpressive.
- Too much to say. There are candidates who feel that they cannot do justice to their many accomplishments and rich careers in one or two pages. To ask them to adhere to such a limit feels confining or slighting.
- Set in stone. Some candidates think that if they put something about themselves in writing it becomes unalterable. If they are still looking at a variety of options, they think that completing a resume will be too binding.
- Not ready to act. Candidates are often asked by their contacts for a resume. Providing a resume to others could mean that the job search is serious and well underway. Not having a resume for distribution can provide a rationale for not yet advancing decisively in job search.

Interviewing

The next topic is interviewing. Most clients recognize that in order to secure a job they will have to be interviewed by prospective employers. So, they accept, in principle, the need for interview coaching and training. There are clients, however, who do not embrace the training wholeheartedly, to put it mildly. For these clients the whole topic of interviewing is anxiety producing. Among the reasons are the following:

- Lack of comfort. Some clients feel awkward and uncomfortable in interview situations, especially when they feel "put on the spot."
- Fear of rejection/embarrassment. Some clients worry a great deal about being rejected for the job or being made to feel embarrassed or ashamed by the interviewer.
- Being put in an overly defensive stance. Some clients experience interviews as a one-way street. They have to answer all the questions and make the grade. They do not approach interviews as a legitimate two-way exchange of information where both parties are evaluating the appropriateness of the job–person fit.
- Hopelessness about the outcome. Some clients feel as if no amount of preparation and effort will make a difference on the outcome. They feel that they will automatically be disqualified from consideration by virtue of their gender, age, physical appearance, lack of credentials, or some other factor.
- Can't compete with outsiders. Clients feel that the job will, inevitably, be filled by internal candidates. How can they compete with individuals who already have a working knowledge of the company? So, why bother?
- The company is just fishing; they are not serious about their interest in me. Clients can feel like the hiring company is only interviewing them because they have worked for a major competitor. The hiring company just wants to use the interview to pump the candidate for information.

Networking

In contrast to interviewing, which most clients accept as inevitable, networking is a topic where many barriers and rationalizations emerge. It is a job search technique that is promoted by most outplacement counselors based on the large percentage of executives who, ultimately, secure jobs based on this method. Yet, it is an approach that poses difficulties, to one extent or another, for a sizeable percentage of candidates. Among the stated barriers and rationalizations for not networking are the following:

- Anger. Clients can be angry about their job loss and about being in a position where they have to rely on networking in order to find a job.
- Don't like asking for favors/using people. Clients can feel like they are "begging" for help when they network. It feels like they have their "hat in their hands." Alternatively, it can feel like they are "using" people they do not know well for narrow self-interest. For some individuals asking for something from others feels like a compromise of their independence.

- Others are too busy. Certain clients assume that other people are too busy to interrupt their work and talk with an individual who is gathering information.
- Fear of rejection. Clients can feel like they will be rejected by potential networking contacts. They assume they will be dismissed in response to their request for a brief meeting.
- Not enough contacts. Clients feel like they do not have a network. They do not know anyone who can be of assistance.
- Contacts are at the wrong level. Clients think that there is no reason for networking because they do not know anyone with the authority to make hiring decisions.
- Contacts are not in the industry of interest. Clients who want to change industries say that they only know people in the former industry. They do not know anyone in the new target industry.
- Contacts are in the wrong geographic area. Clients say that they are new to the area and all their contacts still reside in their former geographic area.
- Damaged goods. Clients feel that nobody who is currently employed will want to meet with them because they are unemployed. Being unemployed means that they are seen as seriously flawed.
- Unwillingness to try "new" ideas. Some clients want to rely exclusively on job search methods that worked for them in the past. They rely on ads and recruiters, for example, despite changes in market conditions since their last search. If ads and recruiters worked in the past, why should I network now?
- It won't work for me/people in my situation. Clients see their situation as completely distinctive and unique. They act as if methods that work for others can not work for them because of their uniqueness or distinctiveness.
- Threatening. Some clients are intimidated at the prospect of networking. Some say that they are just not comfortable and effective in interpersonal situations, whether it is on the telephone or in actual face-to-face meetings.
- Lack of technique. Some clients, of course, need assistance in learning the basic principles and techniques of networking.

Executive Recruiters

Another topic is the use of executive recruiters. There are also a number of explanations offered that prevent clients from using this method. Among them are the following:

- Recruiters are not ethical/too "sleazy." Clients see all recruiters as birds of a feather. They are all untrustworthy and, therefore, should be avoided.
- Fear of rejection or quick dismissal. Clients anticipate being treated shabbily by recruiters and, therefore, avoid them.
- They hurt my chances. Some clients think that all recruiters will overcirculate their resumes. According to this line of thought, overcirculation can lead to several problems. First, the candidate loses control of the job search. Second, the candidate's chances of approaching a company directly are damaged.

- My industry/function is different. Clients think that their industry and/or function is distinctive and, therefore, executive recruiters are not likely to be effective.

Direct Mail

The third major job search technique is direct mail, either in response to published advertisements or as unsolicited correspondence, where candidates write blindly to a company. Here again, there are a number of barriers or rationalizations provided in response to this method. They are:

- Too competitive. Clients think that any ad that appears in a publication will get so many responses that there is no use in even submitting theirs.
- My background is too diverse/too broad. Clients think that the ad calls for very specific qualifications. If their background is too broad or general, it will not match well to the job requirements.
- They are asking for the moon and the stars. I am just a lowly planet. Candidates see advertisements that ask for many excellent qualifications. They feel that because they do not fully match every qualification there is no point in responding.
- Don't write well. Letter writing is seen as a skill area where they are deficient. Their letter, therefore, will not likely have much impact. Consequently, it isn't worth trying.
- Don't know to whom the correspondence should be directed. In the case of unsolicited direct mail, clients say that because they do not know at the outset to whom their letters should be directed, this approach will not work for them.
- Too time consuming. Clients might say that it takes too long to identify the correct individual to whom the unsolicited letter should be directed. Also, it is too time consuming to produce a large number of letters.

Research Materials

The next topic is research using job information sources. Many clients find this topic a difficult one. There are many barriers to using research materials effectively. Among them are:

- Lack of information. Clients might not know where to do library research, and/or how to use the available materials in a productive way.
- Not convinced it is necessary or helpful. Clients might not understand how research can enhance their job search campaign. They think that the really important activities of job search involve face-to-face meetings. Researching is not seen as time well spent.

- Too pedestrian a task. For some more senior executives library research feels like the type of task that they were accustomed to delegating to more junior employees. They feel uneasy, therefore, about having to do it themselves.
- General dislike for library-related research. Some clients have had prior experiences, as students or in business, which left them feeling that library research was time consuming, confusing and unmanageable.

Salary Negotiation

A final job search topic is salary negotiation. As with all the other topics, this one, too, presents barriers to clients. Among the more common are:

- No prior experience. Clients might never have had a job offer where there were elements to be negotiated.
- Fear of losing the offer. Clients might think that, if they negotiate on their own behalf, they might provoke the prospective employer and run the risk of losing the offer.
- Difficulty with assertiveness. Some clients have difficulty being assertive in all situations. Others report the ability to be assertive on behalf of others, but a more limited ability to be assertive on their own behalf.
- Whatever they give me is fine; I just need a job. For some clients the experience of job loss is unsettling, to say the least. They reach the point where the situation feels desperate, and they clutch at the job offer as initially stated by the prospective employer, even if there might have been room for salary negotiation.
- Can't negotiate, market too competitive. Candidates might believe that there is no room for negotiation because it's a buyer's market. The employer can always find someone else to fill the same position. Further, there is a belief that the company is set in its position, bound by strict procedures and salary guidelines.

It should be noted at this time that even though these positions have been referred to as barriers and rationalizations, they are not always purely subjective reactions. There are definitely circumstances where there are elements of reality, perhaps considerable ones, in these positions. Outplacement practitioners need to evaluate each client situation separately and carefully in order to determine how best to respond to these barriers. The next section addresses some of the specific counselor interventions that can be used to address and overcome these barriers.

Major Themes and Counselor Interventions

There are a number of basic themes that run through these barriers around the various job search topics. The first is the lack of information and/or experience. This can refer to lack of concrete information about various job search strategies and techniques. It can refer to lack of information about occupations, industries, and careers. It can also refer to lack of direct firsthand experience in conducting a proactive job search campaign.

Among the possible counselor interventions in response to this theme are the following:

- Directing clients to appropriate library information resources from which clients can learn more about specific occupations, target companies, and industry overviews.
- Encouraging networking so that clients can obtain firsthand information about occupations, companies, and industries.
- Presenting comprehensive workshops where various job search topics are discussed in considerable detail.
- Offering job search teams or groups so that clients who lack information or experience can learn from their more experienced peers. If the counselor's organization does not conduct such groups, assist the candidate in identifying church, synagogue, or community groups who do provide them.
- Providing relevant and appropriate anecdotal information about the job search experience of the counselor's other clients, past and present, so that the candidate can establish a frame of reference.
- Providing relevant and appropriate anecdotal information about the counselor's own job search experiences.
- Suggesting appropriate targeted readings about various job search topics.
- Encouraging involvement with college alumni groups who have a register of individuals who are willing to be contacted for networking purposes.
- Encouraging efforts at partnering with a more experienced job seeker. Some candidates will prefer this one-to-one method to that of joining a group.

In summary, obtaining accurate, up-to-date information in comprehensible, manageable fashion can allow many barriers to be broken. Successful, firsthand job search experiences can also break barriers.

A second theme is the fear of rejection or exposure. Job search involves putting oneself on the line. It is a process where candidates have to consistently get themselves in front of other individuals who will ask them questions about themselves and will, undoubtedly, form impressions about the candidates. Many candidates find it very difficult to be in such a position. There are concerns that they will be judged harshly, evaluated critically and, ultimately, rejected.

Among the possible counselor interventions in response to this theme are the following:

- Reframing. This technique allows candidates to think about the experience of rejection from a different point of view. For example, counselors can help candidates to recognize that a certain amount of rejection is inevitable in the job search process. Candidates need to receive many "nos" before they can receive a "yes." The quicker they accumulate the "nos," the sooner they will get a "yes."

- Or, reframing the rejection in terms of the volume and pace of the job search. More rejections means candidates are generating a higher volume of job search activity. In terms of pacing, if candidates get rejected following a job interview, they can reward themselves for having at least progressed to the point of being interviewed. Much of their competition did not even get to the interview stage.
- Adopting job search strategies that acknowledge the likelihood of rejection and that build in hedges against it. Counselors can discourage candidates from putting all their "eggs in one basket." If they do, and they get a rejection, it feels like they are starting from scratch. Having other "irons in the fire" at all times helps in sustaining momentum.
- Anticipating the rejection and formulating rebound strategies in advance. Candidates can contract with the counselor in advance about a specific response to the rejection when, not if, it arrives. For example, the candidate contracts to send out a certain number of new letters within 1 week of the rejection. Or, the candidate contracts to recontact the decision maker within 1 week of the rejection to elicit feedback in a nondefensive way about the rationale for the company's decision. This allows candidates to position themselves more effectively for the future.
- Understanding more fully the meaning of the rejection for the individual candidate. Rejection will mean different things to different individuals. Each individual has a different history and a different set of dynamic responses to rejection. Counselors cannot assume they know in advance what the rejection means. They must inquire and explore the specific meanings of rejection for each individual candidate.
- Monitoring self-talk. Counselors can explore the self-talk or inner dialogue that takes place within the candidate in response to the rejection. In this way, certain harmful assumptions, if they are operating, can be examined and challenged. This can short circuit the perpetuation of destructive self-talk.
- Acknowledging that it does not feel good to be rejected. The candidate's feelings need to be validated. Rejection is not a painless experience and candidates appreciate knowing that others understand and empathize with their feelings.

A third major theme is that of goal setting. For many candidates, a major difficulty they have in job search is a lack of conviction about a goal or direction. It is commonplace for counselors to hear that the career of certain clients unfolded without a great deal of purposeful planning and goal setting. Inertia was strong and one event lead to another. Job loss, however, often serves as a jolt or a wake-up call. Many are confronted with the extent to which they have drifted. They now face the task of establishing clear goals and directions, possibly for the first time.

Among the possible counselor interventions in response to unclear goals are the following:

- Guiding candidates through a thorough assessment of their skills, accomplishments, interests, values, style, and vocational dreams and/or fantasies. Assessment can be done through a combination of paper-and-pencil exercises and face-to-face discussions.
- Formulating short-term, intermediate, and long-term goals. Candidates need to recognize that career goals are likely to be reached in increments, rather than all at once. Therefore, it is important to build in achievable milestones along the way. This helps to sustain motivation and morale while working toward long-term goals.
- Making sure that goals are defined and measurable. Candidates need to be able to determine how much they have accomplished. They also need to know when their goals have been reached.
- Encouraging candidates to discuss their goals with significant others—spouse, children, friends, relatives—in order to determine how the goals fit with the interests and needs of the others. Enlisting the support of key others is very important, and is less likely if the others are excluded from the goal-setting process.
- Assisting candidates in eliciting feedback from trusted colleagues and peers about what they see as suitable goals for the candidate. Such colleagues and friends might be able to be more objective than the candidate's family members. They are also less likely to be invested in a specific outcome. Their counsel can be very valuable.
- Helping candidates to focus on life planning, not just career planning. What is the relation between the candidate's career goals and the other important areas of life such as family, religion, avocations, community?
- Strategizing with the candidate to identify resources that can be of assistance in achieving goals. Resources can include sources of emotional support, financial support, administrative support, information, advice, contacts.
- Strategizing with candidates about possible barriers to goals. Identifying the barriers or hurdles in advance makes it easier to address them if, and when, they occur. Methods for overcoming the barriers can be discussed. In addition, secondary or back-up goals can be identified in the event that certain barriers are insurmountable.
- Enabling clients to use a variety of approaches in formulating goals. Counselors can assist clients in capitalizing on their preferred methods of problem solving and decision making. They can also encourage clients to use approaches that are less familiar in an effort to enrich the quality of problem solving and decision making. For example, those clients who typically rely heavily on logic and impersonal analysis can be encouraged to also use intuition, fantasy, visualization, and so on. Those individuals accustomed to using intuitive, nonlinear approaches can be encouraged to also use lists of pros and cons, decision-making trees, and other more logical, linear approaches.

In summary, those candidates who have greater conviction about their goals and directions seem better able to motivate themselves in job search than those without such conviction. A major challenge for outplacement counselors is to assist their candidates as effectively as possible in establishing clear goals that can then fuel the career planning and job search efforts.

A fourth major theme is the lack of self-confidence or self-esteem. The experience of job loss can shake the confidence of even the most self-assured individuals let alone those whose self-confidence was already tenuous. Many candidates fear that if they were let go by one employer, then no other employer will ever be interested in them.

Among the possible counselor interventions in response to a client's lack of self-confidence are the following:

- Assisting candidates to become more mindful of past work accomplishments and successes. Often, self-assessment exercises focusing on accomplishments enable candidates to see their skills more clearly. Then, the candidates are better able to articulate their value to prospective employers.
- Enabling candidates to become more mindful of past personal accomplishments and successes. The same type of self-assessment exercises can highlight skills that were used in personal accomplishments. The accomplishments could have occurred in family, community, religious, educational, or athletic settings. Certain of the skills from these accomplishments could be transferred more fully to work settings.
- Aiding candidates in understanding how they have responded successfully to prior setbacks and disappointments. All individuals have developed at least some coping strategies that enable them to rebound from disappointments and failures. Candidates need to recognize how they have done this in the past, so that they can adapt their successful coping strategies to the experience of job loss.
- Encouraging candidates to elicit feedback from family, friends, valued colleagues and peers about what they see as the candidates' strengths, assets, skills, and limitations. This input can be a source of validation and it can strengthen candidates' convictions about what they have to offer.
- Urging candidates to engage in pleasurable activities. For some candidates the temptation is great to deny themselves the pleasure of leisure, recreational, or cultural activities. They feel that they should not be spending either the time and/or money on such pursuits. Job search candidates should not completely forego such activities despite the considerable demands of job search. Such activities can provide much needed opportunities for self-expression, relaxation, stress reduction, relationships with others, feelings of mastery or competence.
- Encouraging clients to focus on other possible bases of self-esteem. Counselors can highlight and support the existing commitments and responsibilities that candidates continue to honor and maintain despite being unemployed. Parenting responsibilities and community involvements can fall in this category.

- Promoting the establishment of social support networks and the linking to community resources. Research has shown that social support can be an important buffer in reducing the adverse impact of job loss (Amundson & Borgen, 1987). Counselors can encourage clients to join social organizations or support groups for those who are unemployed. This enables clients to realize that their thoughts and emotions are not unique, and can minimize feelings of being especially deficient or unworthy. Counselors can also make appropriate referrals to community resources that respond to the financial and practical difficulties brought on by job loss. United Way agencies, educational opportunity centers, and consumer credit counseling are among such resources.

These counselor interventions are suggested in keeping with the proper role of outplacement counselors. It is not the goal of outplacement counseling to alter the deep character structure of outplacement candidates. On the other hand, counselors will be regularly called upon to boost the self-confidence of their candidates in order to facilitate progress in career planning and job search. The interventions are recommended in this context.

In summary, there is an accumulated body of information and experience to which candidates are typically exposed in the course of their experience in outplacement. Althouth many candidates use the information to move forward without great difficulty, others struggle. For many of those who struggle extensively, being provided with concrete information and skills training is not sufficient. Such individuals are confronted by internal barriers or hurdles that hinder their efforts in connection with the various components of job search. The specific barriers can be identified and addressed. There are a variety of counselor interventions that can be used in an effort to overcome the barriers and facilitate productive career planning and job search efforts. In the future, outplacement practitioners will be called upon to become even more skillful at assisting candidates in overcoming these barriers.

Chapter 6

Group Services

To this point much of the discussion has focused on individual outplacement counseling services. However, there is another major format by which outplacement is provided—group outplacement services.

This chapter focuses on group outplacement services. The emphasis is on the rationale, content, and delivery of group services. In addition, there is discussion of some specialized and innovative group approaches to job search.

Rationale

What prompts a sponsoring organization to arrange for group outplacement services rather than individual services? In most cases, the answer boils down to cost. Group services are far less costly. Whereas the fee for a typical full-service individual program might be 10%–15% of the candidate's salary, a group program can be offered for $1,500–$2,000 per day. The group program can typically accommodate up to 15 individuals. So, the cost to the sponsoring organization is roughly $100–$150 per person, per day. As a consequence, by offering group services a sponsoring organization can spread its outplacement budget further. It can provide services to more individuals across broader levels of the organization.

A second reason for offering group programs is location. If the job eliminees are located in a remote area, it is possible that qualified outplacement counselors are not in the vicinity in a way that would make on-going individual counseling viable. Under such conditions, it might be more viable to bring in qualified outplacement consultants for the limited duration that it takes to offer group programs.

What advantages, if any, are there for clients who receive group outplacement services? Amundson and Borgen (1988) summarized the research on group counseling and unemployment. Its major findings suggest that group approaches are well suited to assisting unemployed individuals in the following ways:

1. understanding the points of view of others;
2. developing more effective social interaction skills;
3. learning to share concerns and ideas with others who face similar problems;
4. obtaining a range of reactions to problems that are presented;
5. receiving support and encouragement from others; and
6. obtaining useful information.

Amundson and Borgen conducted one of the few empirical studies designed specifically to identify those factors that were perceived as helpful by participants in job search groups. The helping factors fell into two major categories, those that promoted support and self-esteem and those that facilitated job search tasks. They concluded the following:

> the power of the group in halting a downward emotional slide and moving toward more positive emotional experiences is striking, and this positive stance was maintained long after the group had ended. Even when employment was not found, the unemployed people reported that they were able to maintain a more effective job search and positive self-image as a result of their participation in the group. (p. 113)

Further, Amundson and Borgen concluded that it was important that job search groups begin within the first 3 months of unemployment because many individuals begin a downward emotional slide during this initial period.

Content

There are two major categories of group programs. The first is referred to as the *conventional* group program. The typical conventional group program lasts 2 to 3 days, although there are instances when the program is condensed to 1 day. During that time, the outplacement consultant attempts to present at least a "once over lightly" on the various job search topics. A typical conventional group will address, however briefly, self-assessment, resume preparation, interviewing, job search techniques, research, and salary negotiation. The time devoted to the respective topics will vary from situation to situation, but it is likely that considerable time will be devoted to resume and interview issues. The format will usually consist of a combination of didactic and experiential activities. Opportunities for follow-up, either by telephone or with limited direct access to outplacement counselors, are sometimes provided. The group size is usually limited to approximately 15. Historically, group services were more likely to be offered to nonofficials or hourly employees. However, in recent years, financial pressures have caused many sponsoring organizations to offer group services more widely to managers, as well.

From the perspective of the outplacement consultant, group programs are often seen as a vehicle for breaking into the field. They provide an opportunity for newer consultants to get some valuable hands-on experience under their belt. Most outplacement firms assign their full-service individual clients to their full-time senior consultants. If there are group programs to be delivered, especially in geographically remote areas, firms might call upon per diem consultants. This can be an efficient way for the firm to utilize its counselor resources.

In addition to the conventional 2- to 3-day group workshop, there are some efforts being made to use other group formats more actively in promoting effective job search activity. These other groups are known by a variety of names including *job market attack groups, job teams, job clubs,* or *transition teams.*

The most effective of these approaches bring together the same group of job seekers on a regular basis guided by an experienced outplacement consultant. The groups are based on the rationale that many individuals can do a more effective job search as a member of a resourceful and supportive team than on their own. According to Prichard (1992), a recognized industry expert and proponent of this approach, there are several reasons for the effectiveness of job search teams:

1. candidates receive referrals from fellow job seekers enabling them to expand their networking considerably,
2. candidates attempt job search behaviors that they would not otherwise have tried because they saw it was working for one of their peers, and
3. candidates are pushed by members of the group who saw that they were not doing well and confronted them with that information in a way that got them "unstuck."

There are a number of key issues to consider in forming and running such groups. Membership selection is the first step. Information orientations are often used to explain the group and encourage enrollment. Attention should be paid to the level and background of the candidates. Selection is often done according to job level so that employees who are relative peers work together. Groups are typically integrated by job function and gender.

The structure of the group is important. Group size is typically 8 to 15. Regular attendance is stressed. Cooperation is emphasized and participation is encouraged. Sometimes the group is designed to be time limited with 8 to 12 sessions as a norm. In other instances, the group is designed to be on-going, with arrangements made for new members to be introduced when vacancies exist.

There are a number of activities that form the basis of successful job search groups:

1. Time is spent each week reviewing issues, questions, and developments in the search of each group member. If the group is working well, there will be lots of problem solving, brainstorming, and generating of referrals for one another.
2. Didactic presentations are made by a well-informed leader or group member on topics of mutual interest.
3. Setting of very specific goals for various job search activities (e.g., number of networking meetings, cold telephone calls, meetings with recruiters, ads answered). These goals are posted for all members to view and revisit the following week. Goals and results are tracked publicly in the group, over time, to measure progress.

4. Peak performance training, where group members are taken through a variety of exercises designed to assist candidates in maintaining a positive self-image and in meeting a targeted level of productive activity. The components of the peak performance training include stress reduction, visualization, minimizing the effect of negative events, and maintaining a positive attitude. All of these activities, including the peak performance and the discussion and review of weekly goals, are done in a nonthreatening way, by a counselor who is fully committed to the notion that many individuals can do a more effective job as a member of a team than if they have only individual counseling.

Characteristics of Group Leaders

A few comments should be made about the characteristics of counselors who are likely to be successful in leading groups. In discussing leadership, a distinction can once again be made between the conventional group programs and the job group programs.

There are a number of characteristics that are important for conventional group program leaders. First, the leaders must be knowledgeable about the full range of job search topics including, but not limited to, resume preparation, interviewing, job search techniques, research, and salary negotiation. The leaders must be able to communicate essential information about these topics concisely, as many topics have to be covered in a short amount of time.

Second, the leaders must have at least some basic knowledge about group process and group dynamics. Leaders' responsibilities are similar, in many ways, to that of corporate trainers. They need to communicate a predetermined body of information in easily comprehensible fashion. Yet, the leaders cannot stick entirely to the script. They must know how to field questions, facilitate discussion, and respond to group members who pose special challenges such as a disruptive individual or a withdrawn, nonparticipating individual.

A third characteristic is a high level of energy. Leading a group for 6 to 8 hours per day for several days in a row requires energy, enthusiasm, and the ability to remain interesting to others. Otherwise, it becomes difficult to sustain the active engagement of the group members.

As for leadership of job groups, many of the same characteristics described earlier are important. Certainly, group leaders must be thoroughly knowledgeable about job search topics and have a high degree of energy and enthusiasm. However, there are some additional skills and personal qualities that are central for success as job team group leaders. According to Prichard (1992), the leaders must have:

1. A thorough understanding of group process and group dynamics. Even though each group is different, there are common themes that emerge as group members grapple with issues of job loss in a difficult market. Two issues that almost always surface are how to deal with a dominating group member and how to respond to group members who accept a new job and leave the group.

2. The ability to motivate a diverse group of individuals whose reactions to job loss and job search will encompass a wide range of emotions and a variety of approaches.
3. The flexibility to adopt a number of different roles in the group. Among the roles the leader will typically be called upon to enact are facilitator, coach, teacher, advisor, and expert. Prichard observed that a major limitation of many leaders is that they remain fixed in the expert role, thereby denying group members the opportunity to draw strength from one another and to problem solve effectively with one another.

In summary, group activities are a very important part of the services offered by outplacement practitioners. Group services can be more cost effective for a sponsoring organization, and thereby made available to a wider range of employees. Group services can be offered in a variety of formats. Job team groups have the potential to be very effective in assisting clients in breaking the barriers that impede successful job search activities.

Chapter 7

Physical, Behavioral, and Counseling Implications of the Outplacement Setting

The primary service offered by most outplacement firms is counseling to individuals and/or groups concerning issues of career planning and job search. In addition, most outplacement firms are in the practice of providing office and administrative services to their candidates. The outplacement offices become the base from which many candidates conduct their job search. In effect, the outplacement offices replace the offices formerly occupied by the candidate.

What type of facilities, resources, and services should be provided? According to R. Lee (1987), the offices should be comfortable, functional, and well-appointed. They should be more or less consistent with the type and quality of offices that the sponsoring company provides to its employees. The major difference is that most outplacement candidates who were accustomed to having a private office with the former employer will not have their own private office in the outplacement setting. Outplacement firms have a limited number of such offices and they are, typically, designated for those executives who are receiving the most comprehensive and costly services that the outplacement firm provides.

Most clients find that they can work quite satisfactorily from the library-type carrel or desk space that outplacement firms have. This space is usually available on a "first-come first-served" basis for daily use. Although some clients will initially resist not having their own private office, they typically settle into the available space and find it to be more or less suitable. It is quite possible that the initial misgivings, if they exist, have more to do with clients' feelings about their unemployed status and the symbolic nature of having lost certain of their perquisites, rather than the functional suitability of their new arrangements. For some clients the physical appearance of the offices is so important that it becomes one of, if not the, key criteria in selecting a firm. Consequently, outplacement firms spend considerable resources in designing and decorating their office space in an attractive fashion.

The location of the outplacement offices is an important consideration. Clients like it best if the outplacement offices are near their home, former office, or primary job-hunt area. Commuter access and/or adequate parking are often factors for consideration, as well. Outplacement firms have taken such considerations into account in selecting their office sites. There is a recognition that contracts with large corporations are more difficult to obtain if offices are not well-situated. Securing such prime office space can be very expensive, especially in major urban areas. Effectively managing their real estate costs is a major challenge for outplacement firms. In terms of office equipment, an efficient telephone system is a must, as is an accurate message-taking system. The telephone lines and message-taking services are the candidates' lifeline to prospective employers. Fax equipment, although less common in the 1980s, in the 1990s has become a virtual requirement of outplacement offices.

The capacity to produce job-related correspondence in a timely and accurate way is also critical. Most firms have dedicated word processing personnel to whom candidate materials are submitted for rapid turnaround, usually within 24 to 48 hours. In addition, others have word processing equipment and/or personal computers available for direct client use.

Reference materials are also very important. Most outplacement counselors will stress to their candidates the importance of conducting job search-related research to identify potential targets, to learn more about those targets that have already been identified, and to become better informed about industries and trends. The outplacement firms will typically have at least some basic materials including directories, journals, newspapers, books, and listings. They should also be knowledgeable about additional local resources upon which candidates can draw, such as libraries, chambers of commerce, and universities.

Like many other fields, outplacement has been affected by the rapid expansion of information technologies in the 1980s. Many outplacement firms now feel that it is not sufficient for counselors to merely inform candidates about the value of information resources and then expect them to seek out the materials. Rather, firms are providing on-site access to important databases. Information is available on-line concerning such topics as industry trends, company information, biographical material on key executives, and sources of capital funding. According to Morin and Yorks (1990), there are two major impacts of these new information systems. First, they enable candidates to make stronger presentations and conduct themselves more effectively in job-related meetings. Second, they require outplacement firms to supplement their counseling services with such technological innovations in order to remain competitive.

Finally, outplacement firms, as well as in-house units, need to recognize that they are, at least to some extent, in the hospitality business. Creating a friendly, welcoming environment can contribute to candidates' morale, making it easier for them to maintain good spirits and high energy throughout the job search. Candidates often comment that the atmosphere of the outplacement offices and the treatment they receive from the administrative staff, as well as the counselors, has a definite impact on their ability to maintain a positive attitude.

Behavioral and Counseling Implications of Outplacement Setting

In this section I shift attention away from the mere physical features, resources, and services of the outplacement setting. Instead, I examine a related, but more dynamic, topic. I address the behavioral and counseling implications connected to the outplacement setting. More specifically, I examine the types of client behaviors that can emerge in the outplacement setting, and the ways in which these behaviors can be incorporated into the counseling process in order to facilitate client progress. Special attention is paid to those clients whose job searches turn out to be of very long duration.

Distinctive Nature of Outplacement Setting

The outplacement setting is a distinctive one that presents some special possibilities in connection with professional counseling activities. From a counselor's point of view, it presents the opportunity to observe and interact with a client far more often, and in a wider range of circumstances than one would typically have.

One can think of various counseling settings along a continuum, with differences in terms of how much time the clients spend at the setting and how much opportunity there is for interaction with the helping professionals or the staff. Specifically, in some counseling situations, such as an in-patient unit or a residential facility, clients are full-time members of a setting, living there 24 hours a day. They interact with the professional staff throughout the day and in a variety of different situations. On the other end of the continuum, many more clients participate in counseling activities, whether of a career or a personal nature, on a strictly outpatient basis, by appointment, at the office of the counselor. In this type of situation, the counselor and client see one another for the appointed session, but, typically, do not have any contact between sessions. Their opportunities to get to know one another directly are limited to the designated appointment.

In a curious way, the practice of outplacement counseling usually falls somewhere between these two poles, with certain features of both. This poses some interesting possibilities for both counselor and client.

On the one hand, the outplacement setting is certainly not identical to an inpatient or residential setting. Outplacement candidates are, by and large, a well-functioning population, most of whom have been consistently employed over the years. Their participation in the outplacement services is entirely voluntary. The focus of the assistance they receive is around career issues, not personal issues. They tend to view their situation as transitional, and attribute their unemployed status, at least in the case of job eliminations, to external events. In these ways there are major differences between the outplacement setting and most full-time residential settings where patients are, most likely, more seriously disturbed.

On the other hand, the outplacement setting is not identical to most outpatient situations either. Whereas in the typical outpatient situation counselor and candidate do not see one another except during the appointed hour, in the typical outplacement setting the possibilities for more extensive contact are much greater, depending, of course, on how much time the counselors and candidates spend at the setting. In this way, the outplacement setting is different from the typical outpatient arrangement and contains an element that is similar to full-time settings.

What Can be Learned at the Outplacement Setting?

What is the significance of this opportunity for increased contact between counselor and candidate, and how can it be useful in furthering counseling progress? We turn next to these questions.

It is my contention that this opportunity for increased contact, if understood and applied properly, can be very useful in contributing to progress in outplacement. It provides counselors an opportunity to learn more about the clients and to deepen their understanding of them. This understanding can then be appropriately applied to issues of career planning and job search.

Specifically, counselors are able to learn about candidates, not just on the basis of direct contact with them in individual counseling sessions, but on the basis of candidates' interactions with others, as well. There are any number of questions that counselors can use to organize their observations and guide their understanding of clients. For example, how does the candidate make the initial adjustment to the outplacement setting? Does the candidate move in readily or hesitantly? How does the candidate form relationships with new peers? Does the candidate initiate contact with others or wait to be approached? What type of individuals does the candidate seek out in the setting? How similar or different are they to the candidate?

How does the candidate relate to the support staff? How different is the candidate in relation to the support staff versus the professional counseling staff? How does the candidate organize time and space? How does the candidate spend his or her time at the setting? As time passes, what roles does the candidate take on in the context of the outplacement setting? What part does the candidate play in the group dynamics of the setting? These questions, and many others, can be addressed much more fully by outplacement counselors based on their extensive contact with clients.

A number of specific observations can be made concerning some of the behaviors that candidates demonstrate in the outplacement setting. Although the examples are just meant to be suggestive, they do provide some ideas about behaviors that regularly occur.

There is much to learn about the candidate's interpersonal relations, both with peers as well as with staff. Some candidates report to the counselor in individual sessions that they are interpersonally skillful. They see this as one of their major strengths. In some cases, the counselor's independent observations of the candidate in relation to others is consistent with the candidate's view of self. In other cases, conflicting evidence might present itself. For example, there are some candidates who relate well to peers at their managerial level, but do not form good relations with those at the setting who are of lower or higher managerial levels. Or, there are other candidates who build good relations with the counselor, but demonstrate very different behaviors to the outplacement firm's administrative staff.

The roles in the setting that the candidate gravitates toward can be fertile ground for examination. Some candidates are very helpful to their peers, constantly providing encouragement, support, and leads. Others remain very much to themselves. They neither provide assistance to others, nor ask it for themselves. Their stance seems to be that "I'll leave you alone if you leave me alone." Other candidates quickly take on the role of in-house expert. Having been at the job search longer, they make it a point to pass along their knowledge and experience to the new arrivals. The way in which this is done, and the extent to which their input is welcome, can vary greatly from situation to situation.

Other candidates take on the role of in-house critic. They are quick to identify the limitations of the outplacement setting and its services. They sometimes look to recruit others to their positions, and can spend more time focusing on how to improve the outplacement firm than on their own job search.

Another dimension to consider is how candidates organize themselves, and how productive they seem to be. Some candidates, of course, are highly organized and productive. Calls are made, correspondence is sent, meetings are held, leads are generated. Other candidates equate busyness with productivity. As time passes, it appears that, although they regularly generate a flurry of activity, it does not seem to produce a significant number of substantial leads. Other candidates seem to equate attendance with productivity. They spend long hours at the outplacement setting, but a disproportionate amount of time appears to be spent in nonproductive ways.

Another dimension that can be attended to is a client's ability to maintain a positive attitude. Most job search campaigns have their share of ups and downs. Some clients are able to maintain a fairly even keel, getting neither easily discouraged nor unrealistically overjoyed. Others are subject to wider fluctuations. Some clients rebound quickly from the inevitable setbacks and frustrations. Others take much longer to get themselves reinvigorated. Noticing the manner in which clients manage their emotions over the long haul can be very informative and useful.

Applications of Knowledge Derived From the Setting

Once counselors have made such observations, around these and other dimensions, how can they be utilized to further progress in outplacement? There are a number of possibilities.

First, they can be used for early assessment. Experienced counselors might have seen hundreds of candidates pass through the outplacement setting. They develop an informed perspective about the range of behaviors that clients typically demonstrate. Based on this perspective, they might be in a better position to accurately assess a new client and to intervene effectively as early as possible. For example, a candidate might appear to be rather disorganized and unfocused in the initial counseling sessions. The client does not seem ready to move forward with job search in an active way. If the counselor's contact with the client is restricted to the individual counseling sessions, it might be very difficult to ascertain the nature and pervasiveness of the "stuckness." On the other hand, if the counselor sees the client consistently at the outplacement setting, there might be additional information available that sheds some light. For example, even though the client is disorganized and unfocused in individual counseling sessions, she appears to be making connections with other candidates. She is asking questions of them about their experiences in job search. She is providing them with some information about her background. She is regularly attending workshops at the setting where she is, reportedly, paying careful attention and interacting thoughtfully with the instructor and other workshop members. She is also friendly and respectful toward the support staff.

Contrast this client with another who is also rather disorganized and unfocused in the initial individual counseling sessions. This second client also does not appear ready to move forward with job search in an active way. However, in contrast to the first client, the following is noted by the counselor in observing the second client at the setting. He does not appear to be making any connections with the other clients. He requests an office carrel in a remote corner of the setting. He does not initiate conversations with others, and looks to cut short those conversations initiated by others. He does not attend workshop offerings on various job search topics. He appears to be unfriendly toward the office administrative staff.

Even though both clients demonstrate much of the same behavior in the individual counseling sessions, they are quite different outside the sessions. A counselor who has the opportunity to see these clients in a variety of different situations at the setting will have much more context within which to evaluate the in-session behavior. In this example, the counselor is likely to be much more concerned about the second client. Appropriate interventions can be considered at an earlier juncture, based on the more complete picture.

Providing direct feedback to clients is another very important way in which information generated from the outplacement setting can be used. In interacting with clients or observing them at the outplacement setting, behavioral data is generated that would not otherwise be readily available. The data could be used to confront or challenge, to confirm and validate, or to raise issues for consideration, to name just a few of the possibilities.

For example, Mr. E. was a client who reported to his counselor in individual sessions that his interpersonal skills were strong with individuals at all levels. Yet, his counselor noticed on several different occasions that Mr. E. was very abrupt in his dealings with the firm's administrative staff. The counselor made a mental note of these exchanges. At a later point in the counseling process, as part of a discussion about Mr. E.'s work-related skills, the counselor challenged Mr. E.'s contention that his interpersonal skills were strong across the board. The counselor introduced his earlier observations about Mr. E. and the administrative staff. Mr. E. was able to acknowledge that it was true that, although he typically interacted well with those above him, he was not equally skillful in managing those subordinate to him. A fruitful discussion ensued. Mr. E. admitted that he had been in several different employment situations where those he managed had a high turnover rate. In addition, his staff had low morale and were less productive than expected.

A critical consideration for counselors to keep in mind in such a situation is the amount of trust that exists in the counselor–client relationship. If such observations are introduced prematurely by the counselor, without the existence of a high degree of trust, the client is likely to react defensively. It would be easy for the client to feel like he is in a fishbowl at the outplacement setting. On the other hand, if introduced skillfully at a juncture where sufficient trust exists, the counselor's observations can be very powerful. A couple of elements make them so.

First, they are not based on the client's self report. Rather, they are firsthand observations made by the counselor. In addition, they come from a trusted source. The client has come to trust the counselor as the relationship develops more fully. Third, the observations were made in a naturalistic setting in the course of daily office routine. They provide a glimpse of the client's behavior that is different from what might be seen in the individual counseling session, when a client could make it a point to be on his "best behavior."

Site observations made by the counselor can be used to support and validate, as well as to confront and challenge. Ms. B. was a client in her mid-40s whose self-esteem was shaky. Although a long-service employee who had received a number of promotions over the years, she had difficulty articulating her strengths to the counselor. She focused on her quantitative skills, as well as her attention to detail, in describing those skills that had contributed to her success. Her counselor noticed over the course of several weeks that Ms. B. played a distinct role in the outplacement setting. She took active interest in several new arrivals at the setting. Both of the arrivals were in their mid-20s and were members of the same ethnic minority group as Ms. B. Ms. B. provided encouragement and support to them, and tried to facilitate their orientation to the setting and their new status as job eliminees.

Ms. B.'s counselor introduced her observations at a well-timed moment during a counseling session. This lead to an expanded discussion of Ms. B.'s ability to assist others, something that, it turned out, she had done consistently in managing her staff, but that she had overlooked in her initial discussions about skills with the counselor. Ms. B. gained an increased awareness of her proven track record of having assisted in the development of her direct reports, and was able to use it as an additional selling point in her job search campaign.

Viewing the outplacement setting as a rich source of information about clients has implications for staffing practices. In the examples provided here, several references were made to interactions between clients and administrative staff that were viewed by the primary counselor. In order to capitalize on the full potential of the outplacement setting as a source of information, some organizations include certain key office administrative personnel, as well as counselors, in their staff meetings that focus on client progress. In this way, the primary counselor can receive feedback from the full spectrum of individuals who interact with the client. Although much of the information is often consistent, there are situations where the counselor is provided with much more of a multidimensional description of the client based on the observations of other staff members. In addition, the participation of multiple staff members allows for a more coordinated and integrated approach in dealing with the client. All staff members can be working toward the same goals in their contact with the clients.

The internal Career Services Department of Citibank has used this approach for a number of years. Staff meetings are held regularly to discuss client progress. Certain key administrative staff are invited to attend. All counselors and administrative staff members who have had contact with the client are asked for their input, thus providing the individual counselor with as broad a picture as possible of the client in his or her full range of interactions at the setting. Concerted efforts are made by the department manager and full-time counseling staff in the selection, training, and coaching of those administrative staffers who will be involved in this way. This approach has been consistently successful in providing a primary counselor with important information that can be used to further counseling progress.

Long-Search Clients—The Setting as Nest

Before concluding the section on the counseling and behavioral implications of the outplacement setting, a few comments are in order on long-search clients. Although definitions of what constitutes a long-search client differ, it is fair to say that those who have been at the outplacement setting for a year or more qualify for inclusion. Some of the clients who have been in an outplacement program for a year or more are referred to by outplacement staff as "nesters," for it appears that they sometimes view the outplacement offices as a place of safe and snug seclusion from the outside world.

There are a number of factors that might contribute to a long job search and/or to nesting. Morin and Yorks (1990) cited the following:

- extensive severance pay
- extended employment contracts
- job search campaigns limited to a specific and confined geographic area
- delayed recovery from the initial shock of termination leading to an extended period of denial, anger, or depression
- poor physical appearance
- poor self-image and/or lack of self-esteem
- major difficulty in self-marketing
- tendency to passivity or overdependence on others
- complicating personal or family problem—marital separation, divorce, substance abuse
- litigious posture toward former employer

In addition to these factors, outplacement counselors can use their direct observations of candidate behavior at the outplacement setting to alert them to potential nesters. There are a number of behaviors that individuals demonstrate at the setting that might be an indication of once and future nesting. First, some individuals try to find some physical space at the setting that they can claim as their own. If the firm assigns a permanent office or carrel to clients, they might try and personalize the space by bringing in pictures or desk objects. If the firm typically assigns carrels or offices daily on a "first-come, first-served" basis, the nesters might consistently request the same space. Sometimes, they request space in a remote area of the site, or at least out of the main flow of traffic. Another indicator might be the individual who spends consistently long hours at the site, but who is seldom out of the offices for networking and interview meetings. Such individuals might equate hours spent at the site with productivity in the job search. Most effective job searches, however, balance time spent at the outplacement offices making calls, generating correspondence, and connecting with peers, with time spent out of the offices at networking or interviewing meetings. Another indication might be those individuals who seem more interested in the staff and practices of the outplacement setting, than in their own job search. A disproportionate amount of time might be spent socializing with administrative staff and counselors. Or, a disproportionate amount of time might be focused on discussing the changes that the client thinks could be made in the daily operations of the outplacement setting in order to improve its functioning. In similar fashion, some clients seem to be more interested in the job search activities of others than they are in their own.

Not every client that has a long job search should qualify as a nester. Nor does every individual who demonstrates a few of these behaviors at the outset of outplacement turn out to be a nester. Yet, this is one more way in which behavior demonstrated by clients at the outplacement setting can possibly be used by counselors to get a more complete picture of the client that can then be used to facilitate progress.

In summary, outplacement firms are in the practice of providing office and administrative services to clients, as well as counseling services. The outplacement office setting provides a unique opportunity to learn more about clients across a wide variety of situations and in interaction with a wide range of individuals. The information that is learned can, in the hands of a skilled practitioner, be integrated into the counseling process in order to further job search progress.

Chapter 8

Toward a Theory of Outplacement Counseling

This chapter addresses the counseling theories that guide outplacement counseling. There is very little written about the theoretical underpinnings of the most common counseling approaches in outplacement. This chapter analyzes those models on which outplacement practice is based, and suggests some alternative formulations that are consistent with changes in professional practice.

Many of the counseling approaches used in outplacement are drawn from the field of career counseling. Individual career counseling, along with psychotherapy, can be viewed as variations of personal, one-to-one counseling. One of the interesting and often confusing aspects of counseling and psychotherapy is the great diversity of schools and orientations that exist. Some have estimated that there are at least 100 different forms or approaches (Research Task Force of the National Institute of Mental Health, 1975). Three well-known and quite distinct orientations are psychoanalysis, client-centered or humanistic, and behavior therapy or learning approaches. These three serve as points of reference for the current examination of outplacement counseling.

Behavioral/Learning Models

It is my contention that much of the outplacement approach is based on learning or behavioral models, but that outplacement counseling might be better served with a broader theoretical model. First, certain basic principles of behavioral models as used in outplacement are reviewed. Next, there is a discussion of important contributions that can be integrated from other theories and that can be applied effectively to outplacement work. Although the following discussion of psychological principles might, initially, seem to take the reader far afield of outplacement counseling, its relevance becomes clearer as the chapter unfolds.

Behavioral approaches have traditionally stressed principles of classical and operant conditioning. There is no emphasis on unconscious repressed conflicts or on the importance of very early childhood experiences in understanding the origin of behavioral disorders. Instead, emphasis is placed on environmental characteristics and schedules of reinforcement. The actual performance of the client in counseling and outside the counseling office is highlighted. Social learning and cognitive restructuring are also stressed.

The behavioral approaches view the relationship between counselor and client differently than those of the psychoanalytic or client-centered approaches in at least several major ways. First, they maintain that the relationship can be developed at a faster pace. Although it might take some time for trust to develop, according to behavioral counselors, it can be done rather quickly. This contrasts with the analytic and client-centered approaches where the development of a complex state of "trust" can take weeks, months, or even years. Much of this difference stems from what is meant by the various approaches when referring to the counselor–client relationship. The behavioral counselor is not thinking of a deep bonding or connection, but rather of gaining enough of a working relationship so that the client feels trusting of the techniques being recommended, and for the counselor's interpersonal reinforcements to matter to the client. The amount of trust required is not as great as that required if the client's goal is to consistently search for and reveal hidden and threatening parts of the self, as it is in the psychoanalytic approaches.

A second dimension concerns the effect of the counselor–client relationship on the outcome of counseling. This is sometimes referred to as the *nonspecific factors* by behavioral counselors. Basically, the behavioral counselors get what they can from the relationship in terms of its potential impact on the client, but they do not see the counselor–client relationship as paramount. Procedures, techniques, and information are the raison d'être of good learning-oriented counseling. They are what contributes most to solving the problems that cause clients to seek treatment in the first place.

In this view, the relationship gives the counselor an influence or power base that facilitates appropriate persuasion, reinforcement, use of techniques, and the client's disclosure of details of the problem, so that techniques can be helpfully employed. The combination of techniques and relationship factors gives learning approaches their "double-barreled" effect (Wolpe, 1969). In other words, the relationship is seen as important to the extent that it helps the counselor teach the client to change behavior including verbal, nonverbal, and cognitive behavior. Learning is what is sought, the relationship is not seen as central or as an end in itself.

A third dimension concerns the importance attached to the transference relationship between counselor and client. *Transference* can be defined as a repetition of past conflicts (usually but not always beginning in early childhood) with significant others such that feelings, behaviors, and attitudes belonging rightfully in those early relationships are displaced; in counseling the displacement is onto the therapist (Gelso & Carter, 1985). Another way to conceptualize it is as the repetition in the present of behavioral patterns, feelings, and attitudes that were initially formed in the past. According to the behavioral counselor's approach, the transference is of minimal significance. Although some do briefly discuss transference phenomena

(Ellis, 1984; O'Leary & Wilson, 1975), mostly they are viewed as incidental to the really essential developments in the counseling. That aspect of the counselor–client relationship that does receive the most attention is the *working alliance*. This can be defined as the alignment that occurs between the counselor and client or, more precisely, between the reasonable side of the client and the counselor's working or counseling side (Gelso & Carter, 1985). It consists of an emotional bond between the participants, an agreement about the goals of counseling and agreement about the tasks of the work (Bordin, 1975). For example, one of my outplacement colleagues actually devises a contract with his clients. It spells out in very specific detail the expectations and responsibilities of both counselor and client. It addresses such issues as attendance, scheduling/cancellation of meetings, effort, productivity, agenda for the meetings. These three dimensions then—the degree of trust required in the counselor–client relationship, the effect of the relationship on outcome, and the transferential relationship—are some of the major ways in which behavioral approaches differ from more psychoanalytic and client-centered approaches.

It is my judgment that much of the contemporary practice of outplacement is based, however implicitly, on certain behavioral principles. The next section focuses on the extent to which these principles are useful and valid as guidelines for outplacement counseling.

Fit Between Learning Models and Outplacement

There are many ways in which behavioral-based approaches are well-chosen as the theoretical foundation for the outplacement counseling process. This is especially so for those clients whose search is brief, whose goal is career continuation, and for whom there are few complicated personal or emotional reactions. However, there are a number of ways in which the behavioral approaches might not be sufficient in responding to the full range of counseling challenges in today's practice of outplacement.

Duration of Counseling

First, although it was quite common in the 1970s and early 1980s for executives to find their next job in 5 months or less, more current data suggests that, on average, it takes more than 8 months for executives to secure their next position (J. Aron, personal communication, February 1, 1994). Outplacement firms acknowledge, at least privately, that they have some candidates, perhaps as many as 15% to 20%, who take 12 months or longer. Although there is not a clear consensus about what constitutes a brief counseling experience (Garfield, 1989), it is fair to say that once a counseling relationship has lasted for 9 months or more, it might well take on dimensions more characteristic of a long-term counseling relationship, rather than a brief one.

The nature of outplacement counseling as currently practiced makes the issue of duration a complicated one. Brief counseling approaches typically take one of two approaches to the issue of duration. Some counselors set a specified time limit or number of counseling sessions at the outset. Other counselors might indicate at the beginning a possible range of sessions or a likely termination point, so that the client has a reasonably clear idea how long the counseling will last, thereby diminishing ambiguity about the length of treatment.

Outplacement counseling, on the other hand, is often designed to provide assistance to candidates until they find another position or until they "land," as it is often referred to in outplacement jargon. This unlimited duration is typically referred to as the full-service option. The counselor cannot predict how long the counseling will last given the many uncertainties involved in securing another position. So, for many clients the counseling relationship turns out to be much longer than a brief one, with no assurance at the outset of when it will actually end. In its open-endedness it can resemble a client-centered approach as much as a behavioral approach.

Range of Issues in Outplacement

A second issue concerns the range of topics addressed in outplacement counseling. For many candidates the goal of outplacement counseling is a straightforward career continuation. They are seeking positions comparable to the ones that have been eliminated. They report little desire to explore dramatically different career alternatives. A minimum of psychological assessment is done. Further, the clients report few difficulties in coping with the emotional reactions to job loss and no such difficulties are observed by their counselors. For these candidates the goal of outplacement counseling is to secure a comparable job with the best possible fit in the shortest possible time.

For many such candidates the counseling sessions are very much oriented to learning the various job search techniques and tools. Most of the initial sessions are spent with the counselor instructing clients how to write an effective resume and how to present themselves impressively in interviews. Subsequent sessions might be spent in reviewing the "dos" and "don'ts" of various job search methods including networking, responding to ads, and conducting a targeted mail campaign. Other sessions could be devoted to establishing clear goals and targets for the campaign. Topics such as salary negotiation and the use of information resources are also addressed. The outplacement counseling process is basically one of a counselor providing procedures, techniques, information, guidance, and a modest amount of emotional support.

However, for many clients a much wider range of issues is addressed. For those who undergo a substantive internal assessment process the door is opened to issues of personal style, temperament, values, and interests as well as skills and accomplishments. Implications for significant future change are discussed. With these clients effective counseling can focus on rebuilding self-esteem, gaining new meaning for their lives, and finding an optimal balance of work life and family life. Counseling of this sort requires skillfulness that goes way beyond the mechanics of job search.

Patrick used the outplacement experience to alter dramatically his life circumstances. He was a 55-year-old married officer in the corporate training department of a bank who had earlier careers as a minister and as a teacher.

Both he and his wife had talked for the past 5 years about an eventual relocation to North Carolina. Such a move was seen as a dramatic lifestyle change that would allow for more involvement in outdoor activities such as gardening, hiking, and fishing. However, despite their many discussions, they were not able to follow through with a concrete, action plan. In the face of an unexpected job elimination the situation began to change. Patrick took readily to the outplacement process and quickly developed a strong working relationship with his counselor. This enabled him to do a thorough self-assessment that further clarified his values, interests, and skills. The results of the self-assessment process pointed strongly toward making the lifestyle change sooner rather than later. The full support of his counselor emboldened Patrick to take action where previously he had been stalled. He and his wife made an exploratory visit to North Carolina where she was quickly promised work in her field as a registered nurse. He was able to plant some seeds that later resulted in a training position soon after their relocation. He reported within several months that their lives had changed dramatically for the better. They found themselves able to establish a much more satisfying balance of work, family life, and pursuit of outdoor activities in North Carolina than in New York. Patrick gave major credit to the outplacement experience for providing the impetus, support, information, and guidance that enabled him to change the direction of his life.

Although the heart of individual outplacement counseling involves a relationship between counselor and client, there are some firms and practitioners who also involve the spouse of the outplaced candidate in the counseling process. The spouse might typically be invited to attend a session or two with the outplaced candidate and the counselor in order to learn more about the outplacement process and what the candidate is likely to be experiencing in the months ahead. One national outplacement firm, Janotta Bray, has gone so far as to establish a designated program for spousal counseling for the partners of more senior executives. They estimate that more than 90% of spouses take advantage of talking with those counselors who are designated specifically to work with the spouses. The spouse counseling can last through the candidate's entire job search process (J. L. O'Day & F. K. Woocher, personal communication, April 2, 1993). The involvement of the spouse in this way reflects a broader, more comprehensive view of outplacement counseling. In this respect, it takes more of a family systems approach, and certainly goes beyond what one would typically find in a brief learning-based approach where the spouse is seldom considered part of the treatment unit.

Emotional Support

A third issue concerns the range and type of emotional support that an outplacement counselor can be called upon to provide. Clients can experience a wide range of emotions during the outplacement experience. Anger, pain, fear, sometimes mixed with relief, are just some of the feelings that can accompany job loss. During the course of the job search clients often report feeling like they are on an emotional roller coaster.

The outplacement counselor, therefore, is regularly called upon to help candidates manage a wide range of complicated emotions. Providing assistance in this way requires a degree of counseling skill and sophistication that extends far beyond the nuts and bolts of job search techniques. Helping an individual to express and manage such emotions requires the development of a highly trusting relationship that can open the door to considerable self-disclosure on the part of the client. In this way, also, the counseling relationship goes beyond what one might expect to find in a learning-based approach and resembles more closely the emphasis on counselor–client relationship that one might find in a person-centered or psycho-analytically oriented approach.

Reformulation of Outplacement Model

It has been suggested, therefore, that in some ways a significant number of outplacement counseling relationships do not adhere fully, in practice, to basic behavioral approach principles. These situations require a reformulation of the nature of the outplacement counseling relationship that takes into account the current state of practice. This reformulation would recognize that current practice is sometimes quite different than the original conceptualization of outplacement as a short-term, almost entirely learning-based experience.

An example of such a situation would be that of Suzanne K., a financial services marketing executive in her early 40s. Suzanne wound up meeting with her outplacement counselor for more than 12 months before launching her own marketing consulting business. During the course of those months, the trust between Suzanne and her counselor deepened. She was able to disclose a considerable amount of information about her relationships with her father and an older sister, especially around issues of success, competition, and autonomy. Both her father and sister were very successful in their chosen fields and, as a result, felt justified in advising Suzanne often about her career management. For many years Suzanne had experienced their offerings as intrusive. The insights gained in her outplacement sessions helped Suzanne to realize that her relationships with both her former boss and a key female peer were colored and made more problematic by the legacy of the family relationships. She was also able to gain a different perspective on the conflicts that had developed in her most recent work situation.

The deepened understanding of her career history, in combination with the support of her counselor, enabled Suzanne to seriously consider launching her own consulting business. Then she worked closely with her counselor in exploring the feasibility of a consulting business, developing a business plan, making the decision to move ahead with it, and implementing the early stages of it. The assistance Suzanne received was clearly valuable to her at several levels that exceeded a narrow, learning-based view of outplacement.

Transference in Outplacement

I have contended that individual outplacement can be conceptualized, at least in certain situations, as a counseling activity that goes beyond a short-term, strictly behaviorally based experience. If so, what psychological concepts or principles could then be used to reformulate the outplacement counseling experience in a way that more fully takes into account its complexity? There are many concepts to draw from in the body of knowledge about counseling theory and practice. The concepts of *transference* and *countertransference* are two of them. Although others could have been equally well chosen, the notions of transference and countertransference are discussed because of their long-standing importance in analyzing counselor–client interactions.

Most counselors would probably accept the importance of establishing a working alliance with outplacement candidates characterized by mutual trust and respect. Much more debatable, however, might be the proper way to view the transference or "unreal" relationship in outplacement counseling. The notion of a transference relationship is clearly embedded in psychoanalytic theory, and some view transference as occurring only in psychoanalysis or analytically based counseling. Gelso and Carter (1985), among others, suggested that transference (and countertransference) are universals and occur in probably all counseling relationships. Further, they suggested that transference reactions occur across theoretical orientations and that they occur regardless of the duration of treatment. They occur from the first moment of contact with the counselor, and maybe even before that, as the client anticipates meeting the counselor and the type of interventions to be experienced.

Despite this, however, it is not true that transference occurs in the same way across all kinds of counseling. How it develops, the extent to which it develops at all, and its effects on the counseling progress depend on a number of factors. These include the counselor's view about its place (or lack of it) in the counseling process, the particular client, the particular counselor, and the setting. When working in the context of a psychoanalytic or psychodynamic approach, a counselor might attempt to foster, deepen, and work through the transference misperceptions with interpretations. For example, a counselor might, at a certain point in the treatment, interpret to a client who consistently demonstrates an oppositional style that the client's behavior was shaped in response to a controlling, authoritarian father. It might have been necessary for coping as a young boy in the face of such a figure. However, it is far less appropriate for a mature adult in response to a therapist who is neither looking to control nor dominate. However, in another situation, such as a university counseling center that provides brief therapy to student clients, the counselor might deliberately choose not to cultivate the transference relationship. Rather, the counselor would work with the client around feelings or behavioral change and deal with the transference only if it interferes with the work.

Further, Gelso and Carter maintained that all counselors exert what might be called a *transference pull*. Counselors can never be totally blank screens, however ambiguous they try to be. They always create an image that influences the kind and intensity of transference reactions.

These notions have much relevance for outplacement counseling. Although outplacement more closely resembles the university counseling center approach than the more psychoanalytic approach in the example just provided, there is a need to understand and attend to the transference phenomena in outplacement work. If transference is ubiquitous, then outplacement counselors must at least be familiar with the concept (whether it is referred to as *transference* or *stimulus generalization*), think through the type of transferences that might be triggered by their stance and style, and take steps to address the transferences if, and when, they appear to be interfering with counseling progress. An example might be the white-haired, 60-year-old male counselor who has difficulty building strong rapport with younger clients because his paternalistic appearance and style stimulates in them feelings of conflict they might have experienced with their own father or other authority figures around issues of autonomy and authority. In such a situation the counselor's lack of awareness around the transference pull could lead to breakdowns in the counseling process, especially with younger clients who fit the previous description.

The steps taken by the outplacement counselor in response to transference reactions do not have to involve analytic-type interpretations or addressing the client's early childhood issues in order to understand their origins. Rather, they might involve counselors altering their stance or commenting on the relationship difficulties in whatever theoretical terms are comfortable. An example would be that of a female Caucasian counselor in her 40s who was counseling a similar-aged, Asian, male candidate. She sensed early on that the candidate's cultural legacy around women's roles and male–female relationships in the work place was hindering the formulation of a strong working alliance. She introduced the topic in a way that allowed for a candid and nondefensive discussion focusing on the counselor–client relationship and its potential benefit to him. It cleared the way for a much improved rapport that then contributed to his progress in job search. This was a clear example of how the counselor's grasp of the transference phenomena enabled her to remove a barrier to counseling progress.

Or, attending to the transference phenomena might involve using the manner in which the candidate relates to the counselor as an illustrative model of how the candidate is likely relating to prospective employers or has related to former employers. Many examples come to mind where counselors have held up a mirror for clients to see how their behavior in relation to the counselor is consistent with what they have demonstrated to others in work-related situations. One nonexempt employee, for example, expected the counselor to actually write a resume for him. As this expectation manifested itself in the counseling office, it was used as a lead-in by the counselor to discuss those client behaviors that were seen as passive and dependent by the client's former manager. These passive behaviors contributed to the difficulty this employee had in carrying out his assignment in a rapidly changing environment that required self-starting and individual initiative.

For clients, using the counselor–client relationship as a model for understanding their style and their impact on others can be one of the most valuable and long-lasting benefits of outplacement counseling. In a long-term outplacement relationship the counselor can observe how the client manages time, manages tension, follows through with assignments, responds to setbacks, demonstrates initiative, identifies resources, to name just a few job-relevant skills. In addition, the counselor can assess over time the client's level of interpersonal skill and style in relationship building. For many executives it is issues of style rather than technical competence that spell success or failure in an assignment.

The important point is that counselors need to be trained to recognize transference reactions and respond to them in whatever way is appropriate to the on-going outplacement work. This is a clear departure from behavioral approaches that historically have not had much to say about transference phenomena and counselor interventions designed to foster, understand, or work with them.

Countertransference in Outplacement

One cannot discuss transference without also looking at the closely related issue of countertransference. Epstein and Feiner (1988), in reviewing the psychoanalytic literature on *countertransference* define it as "the natural, role-responsive, necessary complement or counterpart to the transference of the patient, or to his style of relatedness" (p. 293). Some extend the definition even further to include "all feelings and attitudes of the therapist toward the patient." This definition suggests that countertransferential relations are inevitable and ubiquitous for counselors.

Outplacement work is emotionally, as well as intellectually demanding. Regardless of how much self-understanding counselors have, how much insight they possess, or how professionally responsible they are, the emotionally close and demanding nature of outplacement work will trigger responses and reactions in them based on their own psychological history and dynamics.

Examples abound. A common one surrounds the issue of pacing and progress in outplacement counseling. Most outplacement counselors have had the experience of feeling frustrated because a certain client does not seem to be moving forward fast enough. However, when asked directly about the pace of progress, the candidate reports feeling quite satisfied. Nevertheless, the counselor continues to feel frustrated and impatient. In such a case, it could be that the counselor's reactions have much more to do with the counselor than the candidate. For example, it could be that the counselor is made to feel less effective or capable by the slow progress. It could be that the counselor thinks he will look bad in the eyes of his peers or the outplacement firm management. It could be that the client's attitude toward job search progress runs counter to the counselor's characteristic style of taking charge of situations in a purposeful, goal-directed, driven fashion. It could be that the candidate reminds the counselor of others from his past who also frustrated him in this fashion. In short, counselors can easily have a range of countertransferential reactions to their various candidates.

Consequently, rather than viewing these countertransferential reactions as unhelpful and something to be eliminated, it is more useful to view them as something to be attentive to. Outplacement counselors need to be aware of the full range of their reactions to clients, strive to understand them, and be careful not to use these reactions to gratify their own needs. Rather, they should be used in the service of helping clients. If outplacement counselors are trained to recognize the reactions stimulated in them by clients and taught how to use them in the service of the work, it can have a very positive effect on client progress in outplacement. Once again, this represents a departure from traditional behavioral approaches that have very little to say about the impact of countertransferential reactions on the counseling process.

Summary and Conclusion

In summary, the outplacement counseling relationship is a more complicated one than it might first appear given the goal-directed, action-oriented focus of much outplacement work. As such, it is important to understand the counseling relationship as fully as possible in all its dimensions, even those not typically associated with briefer, behavioral approaches. One can make the case that long-term outplacement relationships are similar in many respects to other one-to-one counseling relationships of comparable duration and intensity. Such outplacement relationships might have been initiated without full regard for working alliances or transference and countertransference phenomena. However, at some point, an understanding of these dimensions can facilitate counseling progress.

Outplacement clients have historically been well-served by learning-based, behavioral approaches. It is possible, however, that in certain outplacement relationships, especially those of longer duration and involving a broader range of personal and emotional issues, counseling failures or greatly protracted job searches might result from underattention to the transferential and countertransferential dimensions. Consequently, counselors should be taught to recognize these aspects of the work and be able to work with them when the situation warrants it. This can be done even as the counselor continues to focus primarily on the components and interventions most central to their outplacement goals and objective.

Being trained in this fashion will greatly enhance the skillfulness and flexibility of the counselor. There will be some clients for whom the learning-based approaches will be more than sufficient. However, with other clients, as the outplacement process lengthens, the counselor needs to recognize that "more of the same" (e.g., review of networking techniques, resume revisions, etc.) might not be the answer. It could be that client progress is being slowed by a host of factors that do not concern search techniques or marketplace realities. Counselors with a broad understanding of the counselor–client relationship and an enlarged repertoire of interventions will be better able to reformulate their view of the on-going work. They can then make necessary adjustments that address the relevant barriers and obstacles.

It is my view that outplacement counselors will increasingly be called upon to be much more than job search technicians. Clients seen in outplacement in the future will be an even more heterogeneous group than at present. They will vary in age, race, cultural background, employment and educational level, values, goals, and aspirations. This will pose a substantial challenge to outplacement counselors. The future will belong to those whose understanding of the counselor–client relationship, in combination with market knowledge and job search techniques, allows them to meet these challenges in a knowledgeable, responsive, and flexible fashion.

Chapter 9

Common Patterns of Counselor–Client Interaction

In the previous chapter I stressed the importance to counselors of understanding, as fully as possible, the dynamics of counselor–client interactions.

In this chapter I look at two different approaches for conceptualizing counselor–client interactions. The first approach looks at some of the more common types of problematic clients that are seen in outplacement. It also looks at some of the more common counselor roles. The second approach identifies four different models of counseling and/or helping, and highlights their basic interactional assumptions. It also discusses their relative appropriateness for outplacement counseling.

Problematic Client Types and Common Counselor Roles

A couple of comments are in order before discussing problematic client types and common counselor roles. First, it is important to recognize the limitations of these and all such typologies. All individuals have certain unique characteristics and are never quite the same as the others that might be grouped with them. So, although it is useful for discussion purposes to think about common patterns, it is important not to reify them.

Second, it is important to recognize the interactive, mutually influencing nature of these patterns. The counseling situation needs to be viewed as a two-person interaction, where each individual is constantly influencing and being influenced by the other. So, it is not enough to merely hang a label on the client or the counselor. Rather, it is important to focus on the way in which the client's style and behavior interacts with the counselor's style and behavior in order to produce the counselor–client relationship.

The following, then, is a list of some of the more common problematic client types that appear regularly in outplacement counseling (Bowers & Pickman, 1991):

1. *Passive clients*. These clients are inclined to let others take the initiative for them and their job search. They would like to have the counselor do most of the work of the job search. Their central message is, "You do it for me. I'm helpless. I'm falling apart. Save me."

2. *Help-rejecting clients*. This client type typically comes in one of two varieties. There are those who "yes, but..." their counselors in response to efforts at helping them. Then, there are those who "yes, yes, yes" their counselors, but do not follow through with anything that has been suggested or agreed to. In working with such clients, counselors often feel like they are working harder than the clients at finding solutions.

3. *Entitled clients*. These clients feel that life owes them a lot, and that's how it ought to be. They are owed top-flight outplacement services. Or, they are owed the counselor's total time and attention, or an exceptional compensation package, to name just a few possibilities. The entitled clients also come in at least two varieties. There are the young "fast-trackers" who have never known a major work-related setback, and think that the world owes them a quick and direct route to the senior levels in the company. The second variety are the senior executives who are so accustomed to having people cater to them, that they expect no less from outplacement counselors. At their worst, they treat the counselor almost like a service functionary with very little effort made to establish a bond or connection.

4. *Deferential clients*. Similar to passive clients in some ways, they are more likely to put counselors on a pedestal, thinking that everything counselors say is wonderful and insightful, because the counselors are experts and authorities. The problem is that when their job search stalls, the deferential clients can put the blame on the counselors who, in their minds, should have known better as a result of their greater expertise.

5. *The efficiency expert or scientific problem solver*. These clients place great stock in their logical, analytical skills. They see job search as just another task to be solved using the same logical, analytical approach they use to solve other problems. They often see no need to build personal relationships, either with the counselor or with those people they meet in connection with their job search.

These are just some of the more common problematic types of clients seen in outplacement. Although these brief descriptions do not do justice to the complexity of any given individual, they do contain behavioral elements that are familiar to experienced outplacement practitioners.

At this point we turn to a description of certain of the more typical consultant roles that outplacement practitioners can assume in relation to their clients. Consultants can view their role in a variety of different ways, depending on their individual style, temperament, and background.

The following is a list of some of the more typical counselor roles (M.P. King, personal communication, December 3, 1993):

1. *Facilitator.* Counselors are present to help the clients do their own job search. They see their role as primarily that of enabler or empowerer.

2. *Sounding board.* Such counselors view themselves primarily as a vehicle for assisting clients by listening accurately and reflecting back the thoughts and feelings of the clients so that increased clarity is obtained.

3. *Coach.* Counselors in this role acknowledge that they have some expertise about job search and career planning, but their main goal is to build on and work with the strengths of the candidate.

4. *Teacher.* Counselors in this role view themselves as possessing some important information that they are going to communicate to the clients so that the clients can become more knowledgeable.

5. *Trainer.* Counselors in this role see themselves as possessing a specific plan about how to proceed best in the job search, and their aim is to train the client to follow their plan and use their techniques effectively.

6. *Advisor.* Counselors in this role view the counseling relationship as one in which problems are brought to them by the client. The advisors then help the clients to solve the problems by virtue of their expertise and experience.

7. *Expert.* Such counselors view themselves as the job search/career planning experts. Clients had better listen to their advice and follow their leads. Otherwise, they run the risk of bypassing superior knowledge and experience in this area.

As with the problematic client typology, there are some limitations here as well. No counselor falls neatly into just one of these categories. The more skilled outplacement practitioners are able to draw on a range of these roles depending on the circumstances.

The real value of these two typologies is that they enable us to think more clearly about the counselor–client interaction. With such a frame of reference in mind, the practitioner is in a better position to understand the client more fully and to grasp more completely the dynamic interaction between client and counselor. Problematic interactions can be identified sooner, and well-conceived alternatives can be attempted. Some specific examples can help to illustrate the point.

Suppose a counselor relies heavily on the roles of advisor and expert, and is most comfortable relating to clients in this fashion. Suppose that counselor is working with a client who is a help rejector, whose style is to negate the efforts and suggestions of others. The table is set for a breakdown in the counselor–client relationship. Counselor and client could easily find themselves in a situation of mutual frustration where little progress is made. The client could feel that he is not getting much by way of useful assistance, and the counselor could feel dismissed and rejected. However, if the counselor is able to recognize and conceptualize sooner both his behavior and that of his client, there is an increased opportunity to modify the unproductive interaction in favor of one that is more likely to contribute to counseling progress.

Another example would be the interaction between a very passive client and a counselor whose primary style is that of a facilitator/sounding board. Such a client will likely come to the early sessions expecting the counselor to set the course and do a great deal of the job search work. Specifically, the client might expect the counselor to draft a resume, provide names for networking, and/or names of reputable executive recruiters. The counselor, on the other hand, sees his role as enabling or empowering the client, but definitely not doing things for him. This type of relationship could quickly become very frustrating for the passive client, who might feel that the counselor is not doing enough, not adding much value. The client might become resentful, or might not engage very fully in the outplacement process. However, if the counselor grasps the nature of their interaction quickly and clearly, then the issues surrounding their mutual expectations can be addressed early, paving the way for a much more productive counseling relationship.

A third example would be the interaction between the efficiency expert or scientific problem-solver type client and a counselor whose primary style is that of a coach. Such clients often bring two major beliefs to the outplacement situation. One is that they think the task of job search can be solved by using the same analytical, logical approach that they have historically used to solve other prob-lems. The second belief is that building personal relationships is of much less importance than solving problems and focusing on the task. Such clients often find job search frustrating because it appears to them to be a nonlinear process that often unfolds in an unpredictable way that is difficult to order and control. Suppose such a client is working with a counselor who stresses the importance of building relationships via networking and who finds major satisfaction in the nature of the connections she establishes with her clients. Such a client could easily frustrate her because of his unwillingness to build relationships with others and his lack of interest or ability in genuinely connecting with her. The client could easily perceive the counselor as misguided in her emphasis and not sufficiently analytical in her approach. Once again, an early recognition of their respective styles by the counselor holds out the potential for their reactions and preconceptions to be addressed, thereby paving the way for a more productive counseling relationship.

Four Models and Outplacement Counseling

Next, we turn our attention to four models of counseling and helping that are potentially relevant to outplacement counseling. The models were developed by Brickman et al. (1982). The models highlight assumptions held by both counselor and client that might also be embedded in institutionalized programs of assistance. These models are another way of conceptualizing the counselor–client interaction in outplacement.

The four models are as follow:

1. *The moral model.* In this model, individuals are assumed to have responsibil-ity for both creating and solving their own problems. This model rests on the

assumption that clients got themselves into their dilemmas and they can get themselves out of them. Counselors typically take a direct, confrontative, authoritative approach to helping others when operating on this model.

2. *The compensatory model.* In this model, individuals are not blamed for their problems, but they are expected to be responsible for the solutions. Individuals are expected to compensate with extra effort, intelligence, or constructive use of others to change the problems or dilemmas imposed on them. In other words, individuals' problems are attributable to external factors beyond their control, such as poor upbringing, cultural disadvantages, traumas, or corporate decisions to downsize. The counselor's role is to provide remedial help in assisting the individuals to help themselves.

3. *The medical model.* In this model individuals are not responsible for either the problems or the solutions. This model is reflected in the traditional medical relationship where patients are seen as victims of infection or physical malfunction. Only the physician can cure the problems. This model allows individuals to request help without blaming themselves. However, it also fosters dependency.

4. *The enlightenment model.* In this model individuals are responsible for their problems, but cannot be held responsible for the solutions because the problems are too difficult to solve alone. In this model individuals are expected to "accept a strikingly negative image of themselves and, in order to improve, to accept a strong degree of submission to agents of social control. It is their own impulses—to eat, drink, steal, etc. —that are out of control. They are expected to submit to the stern or sympathetic discipline provided by members of the community in order to control the impulses" (Brickman et al., 1982, p. 375). Alcoholics Anonymous, for example, is a program that is designed along these lines.

According to Morin and Yorks (1990), a clear understanding of these four models can assist counselors in recognizing the extent to which they are operating on similar assumptions as candidates and to what extent they might be at cross purposes. Using this framework, issues concerning the counselor–client relationship can then be addressed more effectively.

For the most part, according to Morin and Yorks, outplacement counseling is based on the compensatory model and to a lesser extent on the moral model. The compensatory model posits that in the case of job eliminations, it was really not the candidates' fault that the jobs were lost, and with hard work they can find others. The emphasis is placed on getting candidates to understand what happened and to accept responsibility for future action, not on blaming or faulting them for past actions.

The moral model posits that candidates selected the company, remained in the situation, behaved in a certain way and, therefore, should not complain about being let go. Further, the candidates now need to find themselves another job. Counselors might find it necessary or helpful to use this approach, especially to shake a stuck client, but are advised to do so judiciously, as it might cause the candidate to feel unsupported or abandoned.

The compensatory and moral models are seen as most appropriate for outplacement counseling because they embrace the basic notion that clients are ultimately responsible for making use of the counselor's help in securing employment. In this process the client's competence is reinforced. The other models either foster dependency by minimizing the client's need to take proactive steps or promote an overreliance on a strict, authoritative structure or figure.

In summary, it is important for practitioners to understand the counselor–client interaction as fully as possible, especially with more problematic clients. Two different approaches for conceptualizing counselor–client relationships were discussed. The first approach identified a brief typology of problematic clients and described typical counselor roles. The second approach identified four different models of helping and highlighted the assumptions upon which they are based. Both approaches enable practitioners to understand the dynamics of counselor–client interaction more fully, thereby paving the way for a more productive outplacement experience.

Chapter 10

Is Outplacement Ever Therapy?

One of the more subtle and delicate counseling issues in outplacement is the relation between outplacement and psychotherapy. It is important that counselors examine and understand this issue carefully. The more fully counselors understand the relation between outplacement and therapy, the greater the likelihood that their outplacement counseling will be guided by a sense of appropriate boundaries and parameters.

Outplacement counseling was defined at the outset of this book as a process of helping employees who have been terminated or whose jobs have been eliminated to face their job loss with renewed self-confidence, to learn effective job search strategies and techniques and to conduct a successful job search campaign. If the focus were exclusively on the learning of effective job search strategies and techniques, there would be very little to discuss concerning the boundaries of outplacement. However, because outplacement counselors assist individuals in renewing their self-confidence and support them through the emotional ups and downs of job search, the issues become more complicated.

Should Psychotherapy Precede Outplacement Counseling?

A first issue concerns the appropriate sequencing of outplacement and psychotherapy. There are times when psychotherapy should precede outplacement. There are other times when the two can proceed simultaneously.

When they first meet, outplacement counselors must determine the extent to which candidates are ready to engage in an outplacement process. This requires assessing the candidate's reaction to termination or job elimination. Is the reaction transient and sufficiently mild to allow outplacement to begin? Or, is the candidate overwhelmed in a way that prevents any current benefit from outplacement? In most cases, candidates are able to benefit from outplacement as soon as possible.

There are at least two situations, however, that argue against the initiation of outplacement counseling. The first is a situation involving active substance abuse. Clients who are abusing alcohol or drugs should not begin outplacement counseling, as they are not in sufficient control of themselves. They are unlikely to benefit from their discussions with the outplacement counselor, and the demands of conducting a job search could expose them to an overwhelming level of stress. Further, it is also inappropriate to have an active substance abuser at the outplacement site. It is potentially disruptive to other candidates and communicates the wrong message about the type of behavior that is acceptable at the site. If outplacement counselors learn of a substance abuse problem, they should be prepared to facilitate referral to appropriate service providers.

A second situation is the candidate who is severely depressed or acutely anxious. Once again, this is a situation where the candidate is unlikely to benefit from outplacement counseling. In the case of depressed clients, they are unlikely to have available the energy, motivation, and sense of purpose to conduct an effective job search campaign. In the case of clients overwhelmed by anxiety, they are unlikely to maintain the focus and clarity to initiate and conduct an effective search.

Outplacement or Psychotherapy? Or Both?

There are probably a much larger number of cases where it is perfectly advisable for candidates to begin outplacement counseling, but where it becomes clear sometime during the outplacement process that additional professional assistance is in order. This is the type of situation where the relation between outplacement and psychotherapy can become very delicate and subtle.

Although each situation must be evaluated on its own terms, there are some general considerations to keep in mind regarding the relation between outplacement and psychotherapy. These considerations will help the outplacement counselor to determine whether a recommendation of referral to psychotherapy should be made.

One consideration is prior level of functioning. What was the candidate's level of functioning prior to the job loss? How motivated was the candidate? How energetic? How capable of carrying out complex projects? How has the level of functioning been influenced by the job loss?

In many cases, candidates will report having functioned very effectively prior to job loss. The job loss then contributes to some disruption in the client's functioning. However, with some effective counseling and coaching candidates resume their normal level of functioning relatively quickly.

In other cases, however, candidates are not able to move forward effectively in job search. They attribute their difficulties to the effect of job loss. In such cases, it is important for the counselor to have an accurate picture of the candidate's level of functioning at work prior to the job loss. The job loss might, indeed, be responsible for the difficulty. It is also possible, however, that the job loss merely served to surface some long-standing difficulties. This is a situation where a discussion about possible referral for psychotherapy might be in order.

There is a second situation where the relation between outplacement and psychotherapy surfaces. It revolves around the nature of the difficulty a candidate is having in moving forward with job search.

There are at least three major areas to consider in effective career planning and job search. The first is self-assessment. Candidates need to have a grasp of their skills, accomplishments, interests, style, and values. The second area is external assessment. Candidates need to be knowledgeable about various industries and occupations. They need to understand the conditions of the industry and the demands, requirements, and satisfactions of various jobs. Understanding both themselves and the world of occupations allows an individual to set career goals with the conviction that the goal is a well-chosen one. The third major area is that of job search methods and techniques. Once having established a goal, the candidate needs to know how to carry out an effective job search campaign.

If an outplacement candidate is experiencing difficulty in job search it is important for the counselor to determine the basis for the difficulty. It could rest in any one of the three areas—knowledge of self, knowledge of the world of work, or knowledge of job search methods and techniques. It is also possible that a candidate is quite knowledgeable in all three areas, but is still stuck in his or her job search. In such cases, it is important to consider what barriers or hurdles might be interfering with the candidate's ability to move forward. It is possible that the barriers are not informational in nature, and will not be alleviated with additional testing, information gathering, or reviewing of methods. Rather, the barriers might be more emotional in nature and, consequently, require the intervention of a mental health professional rather than that of the outplacement counselor.

Establishing Appropriate Boundaries

How does the outplacement practitioner determine how far to go in establishing appropriate boundaries between outplacement counseling and psychotherapy? How far should the counselor go in exploring candidate issues that might be better left to psychotherapists?

One guideline that seems to work well is to always maintain focus on the career-related connections of the issues under discussion. In other words, counselors should have a well-considered rationale for probing into client concerns of a more personal nature. The rationale should be based in the relevance of the inquiry to career-related matters. Counselors need to have a good idea how the information they might elicit will help address the client's career issues. Probes should never be justified by mere curiosity on the part of the outplacement counselor. Nor must the inquiry be done to indulge outplacement counselors in any fantasies they might have of practicing psychotherapy. It is appropriate to explore whether emotional factors are impacting on job search. It can be appropriate to identify what those factors are and to highlight the consequences of those factors on career management and development. It is not appropriate, however, to explore in any great detail the psychodynamic origins of those factors. Nor, is it appropriate to treat them in a way that exceeds the skill and training of the outplacement counselor.

There is another, although far less frequent situation that involves the relation between outplacement and psychotherapy. Some candidates will inform their outplacement counselors that they are already in psychotherapy and that their treatment has preceded job loss. The outplacement counselor should, in general, be supportive of the candidate's psychotherapeutic relations, especially given the stresses associated with job loss and job search. Some outplacement counselors will occasionally look to coordinate their efforts with those of the therapist via professional consultation. This should only be done following a discussion with the candidate where permission is granted, and then, only if the outplacement consultant feels competent in such a role. Great care must always be taken to ensure that clients do not feel like the confidentiality of their therapy relationship is violated.

There is yet another way in which the relation between outplacement counseling and psychotherapy is complicated. It relates to the content of individual sessions. Many topics can emerge in the course of a counseling session. Some are clearly job search related such as discussions of interviewing, networking, and resume preparation. Other topics are broader, but still clearly job search related, such as the impact of job loss on a candidate's family. At other times, however, candidates might discuss concerns or frustrations whose relevance to job search is not readily apparent to the counselor. At such moments the meeting can feel to the counselor like a "therapy" session. Knowing how to respond requires skill and judgment. In some cases, clients might need to ventilate or decompress for a brief period in the presence of an empathic listener. Having done so, the clients are then able to turn full attention to job search matters. To have interrupted the ventilating prematurely would be disruptive to the counselor–client relationship. At other times, however, the ventilating and decompressing seems like it could go on and on, and the candidates appear unable or unwilling to refocus on job search matters. Knowing how to respond in the most effective way to this situation in order to keep the services within the appropriate boundaries of outplacement is an ongoing challenge for practitioners.

In summary, the relation between outplacement and psychotherapy is a delicate one. Outplacement counselors should strive to understand the relation between them to ensure that candidates receive the most helpful and appropriate assistance available. Counselors must always practice within the scope of their skill and expertise, and in a manner that is within the appropriate boundaries of outplacement. They should also be mindful that although outplacement is not therapy, it can be highly therapeutic to individuals experiencing one of life's major stressors.

Chapter 11

Background Qualifications

This chapter addresses issues concerning background and training qualifications needed to work effectively as an outplacement counselor. Although there is no single set of criteria on which all would agree, there is some common ground. There are several areas to consider including skills, experience, education, and personality or attitude.

Skills and Knowledge

We begin with a discussion of the skills and knowledge required to work effectively as an outplacement counselor. Milligan (1992) addressed this issue on behalf of AOCF. The outplacement practitioner must have good counseling skills. At the heart of counseling skill is the ability to listen accurately and to understand the messages and feelings of the client. The outplacement counselor should understand thoroughly the candidate's abilities, interests, values, and experiences, and be able to communicate that understanding back to the client.

The counselor needs to be knowledgeable about tests and assessment tools. Assessment is useful in gaining as complete a picture as possible of the client so that clients are in a position to make more informed decisions about their job, career, and lifestyle. When conducted by a skilled practitioner, assessment is also important in promoting enhanced self-esteem in the client. Counselors must recognize, however, the limits of their competence in this area and perform those functions for which they are qualified.

The counselor needs to be an expert in the job search process. There are a wide variety of techniques and approaches that can be used to assist an individual in conducting a job search. The counselor needs to have as large a repertoire as possible, as no two job searches will be identical. Experience and knowledge gained over time will help the counselor to determine the best techniques and approaches for a particular client.

The counselor needs to be knowledgeable about industries, job functions, and the world of work. Although it is impossible for an individual counselor to have expert knowledge about more than a handful of industries or occupations, it is important to remain as informed as possible about a wide range of major trends and developments. This will enable the counselor to be more effective in assisting the client in career planning, targeting, and decision making.

Knowledge about information resources is very important as well. Clients can benefit greatly from an effective use of the various resource materials, directories, journals, databases, associations, company reports, and so on, that exist. These materials enable the candidate to learn more about companies that have already been targeted or to identify additional targets. Counselors need to be able to assist clients in this way.

Excellent communication skills are critical for the outplacement practitioner. Strong writing and editing skills are necessary in order to assist clients in developing resumes and cover letters. Strong presentation skills are critical as well. Many clients need help in promoting themselves effectively to networking contacts and prospective employers. The counselor needs to be able to provide specific feedback about the client's self-presentation and to model effective alternatives. The use of role plays and videotape equipment can be especially helpful in this regard.

Counselors must also be able to motivate candidates consistently. Inevitably, certain candidates get bogged down in the job search process and find it difficult to sustain a high level of effort and application. The counselor is often seen by the several interested parties—corporate sponsor, outplacement firm management, and candidate—as a source of motivation and inspiration. Counselors must be able to sustain this ability even in the face of large caseloads and protracted job searches.

There is another dimension that is very often valued in outplacement counselors. It concerns the manner in which they present themselves. It is most often referred to as a *corporate presence* or *corporate appearance*. Although it is not easy to define, it usually refers to a certain style of dress and comportment that communicates that the counselor is knowledgeable about corporate cultures and mores. This corporate presence adds to the counselor's credibility in the eyes of candidates, most of whom want to be reassured that their counselor understands the world from which they came.

Strategic marketing and planning skills are also very important for the counselor. Clients typically need assistance in developing an overall job search campaign plan including an effective marketing strategy. The strategy must help the candidate determine how to set himself apart from the competition. Although this list is not exhaustive, it does include most of the core skills without which effectiveness as an outplacement counselor is likely to be limited.

Background and Formal Training

What type of education is necessary in order to be an effective outplacement practitioner? Once again, there is no unanimity on this issue among practitioners. In this category, there are some widespread differences of opinion, reflecting the varied backgrounds from which outplacement practitioners have come. As is so often the case, individuals tend to place great stock in their own experiences and see them as worthy of emulation. Specifically, there is a large group of outplacement practitioners whose background experience is primarily in large corporations. They value this business experience above all else, and think that formal counseling training is less important. According to this view, counseling skills can be learned or have already been learned by those who have good interpersonal skills. This group is more likely to view their role as that of coach, advisor, or business consultant. They are more likely to take a problem-solving view of outplacement work.

On the other hand, there is also a large group of practitioners who come to outplacement from a background that includes formal training in counseling. They are more apt to see counseling as a very specialized set of interpersonal skills, and one that requires some specialized training. They are also more likely to attach considerable importance to the process, as well as the outcome, of outplacement counseling. They are more likely to see counseling as a two-way mutually influencing interaction. It requires the ability to understand and examine critically the counselor's contribution to the interaction as well as the candidate's. Chapter 8 provides a more in-depth discussion of this view of the counseling relationship.

The optimal background for an outplacement practitioner is one that combines both relevant business experience and specialized counseling training. One needs to be knowledgeable about the corporate world in order to be credible and helpful to clients. In addition, one needs to be skillful in counseling in order to meet the challenges of outplacement.

Being multidimensional in this way has a number of advantages for practitioners. One of the major advantages is that counselors are not as limited with regard to the type of clients with whom they work effectively. Practitioners have a tendency to get somewhat typed within their own outplacement firms. For example, certain counselors are seen as "savvy business types," whereas others are seen as "highly skillful counseling types." Candidate assignments are often made accordingly. The savvy business types get the very business-type candidates, whereas the highly skillful counseling types get the candidates who pose more obvious counseling challenges. Although such a practice appears proper from a counselor–client fit perspective, it can be limiting from the perspective of the counselor's long-term professional development. If the counselor is seen in a rather one-dimensional way and assignments are made accordingly, the counselor's range of skills might not be expanded. However, if the counselor has both business savvy and excellent counseling skills, a wider range of client assignments can be made, and the possibility for professional growth and development is enhanced.

Another interesting dimension of the discussion about counselor experience and background concerns the extent to which the counselor's experience has to match that of the client. Specifically, is it important that the counselor have been through a job elimination or termination in order to understand the client's experience? In the early years of outplacement there are some who would have argued so. The thinking was that only those who have been through the experience can truly understand the clients and be empathic toward them. This is too narrow a view. The focus should not be on whether the counselor has been outplaced. The more significant issue is to what extent counselors have experienced major transitions in their life. The transitions might have taken a variety of forms—job loss, death of a loved one, divorce, career change—its specific details matter less. What matters more is having experienced loss and change and the many complex feelings that accompany them. The firsthand experience of struggling actively with change and recognizing the process one has to go through in order to move forward is key. Such direct experiences enable the counselor to be more understanding, empathic, supportive, and credible to those who have experienced job loss.

Having said all this, it is important to add that counselors need to guard against overgeneralizing based on their own experience. It is not helpful to assume that all others experience change exactly as we do. Effective counselors are those who can both draw on their own experiences to understand others more fully, but who recognize the that no two people have identical experiences. There must be a healthy respect for individual uniqueness and separateness even as we seek common ground.

Personal Attributes

A final area for consideration is personality or attitude. There are a number of desirable personal qualities for outplacement practitioners. Gallagher (1982) cited several such factors. One is genuine respect for other people, especially those whose values differ from those of the counselor. The ability to respect individual differences, already a critical attitude for effective counseling, will become even more important in the years ahead. Clients seen in outplacement in the future will be an even more heterogenous group than at present. They will vary in age, race, cultural background, employment, educational level, values, goals, and aspirations. In order to be effective, counselors will have to build relationships of trust where such differences exist. Respect for the differences will be a must.

Another quality that outplacement practitioners must possess is curiosity. They need to be curious both about themselves and the world around them. The work world is undergoing very rapid changes in many areas. These changes are influencing our methods of production, distribution, communication, organization, to name just a few. We know that these changes have affected, and will continue to affect, the careers of individuals. Yet, it is not entirely clear in what ways this will take place. So, outplacement practitioners must be consistently inquiring and observing, in order to determine how best to help their clients respond to these changes.

Counselors must also remain curious about their own counseling approaches and style. It is only by doing so that they can understand fully the impact they have on their clients and can maximize their role as change facilitator. In other words, outplacement counselors need to be knowledgeable about developments at multiple levels of analysis: individual behavior, dyadic interactions, group trends, and societal changes. This is a tall order that requires a curious, inquiring attitude.

Breaking Into Outplacement

Having discussed the background and training qualifications needed to work effectively as an outplacement counselor, a few words are in order about the means by which practitioners actually enter the field.

There are a variety of methods by which the field is entered. Historically, the field had what is commonly referred to in the literature on occupations as *low barriers to entry*. In other words, it was relatively easy to get started. There were no licenses or regulatory requirements. Entry was possible from a variety of different background fields. This made it relatively uncomplicated for some early practitioners to start their own outplacement firms or to approach existing firms about employment opportunities. Most of the early practitioners had substantial work histories either in corporate settings or in counseling/education settings. Consequently, some firms developed attaching greater importance to business experience, whereas other firms developed attaching greater importance to counseling experience. Presently, any aspiring outplacement counselors would do well to understand the orientation of the outplacement firms with whom they are interviewing. Specifically, evaluating whether the firm and its decision makers are more business-oriented or counseling-oriented will assist the would-be counselors in determining whether a good job–person fit is likely.

Another dimension about entry concerns the basis on which counselors are hired. Outplacement firms quickly learned that flexibility in staffing was a key to their success as viable business entities. The nature of their assignments was difficult to predict and control. If the firm received a large contract from a major corporation, there could be a sudden need for an expanded number of counselors. However, during slower periods it was not necessary and, from a purely business point of view, unprofitable to have the same number of counselors on staff on a full-time basis.

The model that evolved was that of a two-tiered approach that characterizes the staffing pattern of most outplacement firms today. One tier is the full-time permanent core of professionals. The other tier is the group of nonpermanent professionals who are referred to by a variety of descriptions such as per diems, stringers, or associates. Typically, the larger outplacement firms will periodically train a group of per diems in the firm's methods and approaches to outplacement. Having been trained, the per diems are then seen as "bench strength," players who can be pressed into service if a new or current assignment warrants it.

A few words are in order about the nature of the training that is provided by the outplacement firms. Although there are, undoubtedly, some firms that are more thorough than others, the training is, for the most part, rather brief. Would-be practitioners would do well to not assume that everything they need to know about delivering high-quality outplacement services will be taught to them in the firm's training program.

Staffing in this fashion meets a couple of outplacement firm objectives. First, it reduces fixed staffing costs by keeping to a minimum those employees who are full time and for whom full wages and benefits are provided. In addition, it allows the firm greater control over the location and flow of its employees. Specifically, it means that firms can keep their core staff closer to the home offices and can staff projects in remote areas with per diem employees. Having this type of flexibility can be important in maintaining continuity and access in counselor–client relationships. In a related development, some national firms are now in the practice of subcontracting with regional or local firms and individuals for out-of-town assignments. This frees the national firms from having to send a team of its own people to the location.

How then does a prospective professional enter the field today as an outplacement counselor? There are several routes by which it happens. Some individuals without prior outplacement experience are hired as full-time permanent counselors. They tend to be more established individuals whose breadth and depth of corporate experience brings immediate value to the outplacement firm and outweighs their lack of prior experience. For example, several such individuals who have been hired by major outplacement firms were senior human resources executives for many years in large corporations. They convinced the outplacement firm hiring managers that their senior corporate experience and presence would enable them to work well with the firm's more senior candidates. In addition, they had many contacts at the senior human resources level at other major corporations, a source of potential business for the outplacement firm.

Many other would-be counselors are invited by the firm to complete its training program, and then, sooner or later, receive initial assignments to provide services on a per diem basis. Very often these initial assignments are to deliver group workshops on location at the sponsoring organization. The initial assignments can, however, involve individual counseling as well. Then, based on the counselor's performance and the firm's contracts, additional assignments can be made.

Another route by which some individuals begin practicing outplacement counseling is by way of a two-step process. In such cases an individual might be hired by the firm based on a desired noncounseling skill or experience. Both parties might then agree that at some designated point in the future the individual would have the opportunity to provide counseling services as well as, or instead of, those services for which he was originally hired. Specifically, a number of practitioners were initially hired as marketers or business development professionals. They then later made the transition to counselor. Another colleague was originally hired by her firm as the in-house information specialist, and eventually crossed over to counseling.

Whichever of these routes aspiring counselors pursue, there are a number of activities that can enhance their prospects. Like any other job seekers, they should become as informed as possible about their targeted field. This can be done in a number of ways including networking with current practitioners, attending chapter and national IAOP meetings, reading any available literature on the field, enrolling in training experiences that can enhance relevant skills, to name just a few.

In summary, those who become successful outplacement counselors must possess a wide range of skills, abilities, and personal attributes. Although current practitioners come from a wide variety of backgrounds, most possess some combination of business and counseling skills. There are also a variety of routes for breaking into the field.

Chapter 12

Professional Development

This chapter focuses on issues of professional development for outplacement counselors. It begins with some discussion of the historical and sociological conditions that have generated increased interest among practitioners in issues of professional development. It then addresses some of the symptoms that practitioners might experience that alert them to the need for further professional development. Closely linked to the symptoms are the work-related stresses that can limit effective functioning of practitioners. Finally, this chapter addresses a variety of ways in which outplacement counselors can act to enhance their professional growth and development.

Growth of Interest in Professional Development

As the earlier section on the history of outplacement made clear, the outplacement industry is a relatively new one. Much of the effort in the early years of the 1960s and 1970s was spent in establishing and launching the industry. The 1980s was a period of rapid growth and expansion. Although precise statistics do not exist, many outplacement practitioners entered the field in the 1980s. The Gallagher (1990) survey of outplacement practitioners, conducted in 1990, supports this observation in noting that the average number of years in practice for his 300 respondents was approximately 6. For much of the 1980s, issues of professional development did not loom as large because, for many practitioners, the field was new and expanding. There were lots of challenges that required rapid learning in order to meet client demands. In effect, many practitioners were fully engaged in learning the basics of their trade "on the fly."

However, things began to change as practitioners put more years of firsthand experience under their belts. Many of the basic outplacement approaches and techniques became much more familiar. The learning curve for many practitioners began to level off. As a result, more questions began to be raised among practitioners about how they could continue to grow and develop as they and the industry began to mature. These discussions coincided with the establishment of the IAOP in 1989, with its stated mission of "serving, supporting, *developing* and uniting" individual outplacement practitioners. Much of the rapid growth of this grass-roots organization was attributable to its responding to the needs of individual practitioners for a forum where issues of professional growth and development could be addressed and where opportunities could be made available for ongoing professional education.

There is another factor that might account for issues of professional development emerging more fully at this time. It is related to the career sequencing or pathing of outplacement counselors. Many of the earliest practitioners of outplacement were individuals who already had lengthy work histories. Many were males in the 50- to 60-year-old range. Having some grey hair was, in many quarters, seen as an occupational asset.

Outplacement was viewed by some of these earliest practitioners as a second career that could cap an already substantial corporate work history and serve as a bridge to retirement. They projected being involved in outplacement for 10–15 years. Under these circumstances, issues of long-term career development did not loom so largely, for either the practitioners were not going to be in the field that long and/or there was no need to consider how a stint in outplacement would bridge them to a subsequent career.

However, as younger practitioners entered the field, issues of long-term career development began to loom larger. A practitioner entering the field at 40 might be spending 20–25 years in outplacement or subsequent careers. From this perspective, issues of long-term career development became more salient and needed to be addressed more fully.

Another set of considerations that generated strong interest in professional development were the changes in marketplace conditions and their effect on candidate job searches. Beginning in the mid- to late-1980s outplacement practitioners found that, on average, it took their candidates longer to secure new positions. Counselors recognized that they needed to become even more skillful about career planning and job search to be of maximum assistance to their candidates under these difficult marketplace conditions. This spurred interest in professional development opportunities.

Another major reason that professional development issues became more salient is that dedicated counselors began to recognize that the price of not developing professionally could easily be a loss of enthusiasm, motivation, and satisfaction from their work in outplacement. If such a trend continued unabated it could lead to professional burnout.

Potential Burnout Among Outplacement Counselors

This section examines some of the symptoms that can emerge if counselors begin to lose enthusiasm for their work. It also discusses some of the stressors characteristic of outplacement counseling that can contribute to the loss of enthusiasm and, potentially, to burnout.

Before beginning, a few comments about definitions are in order. Much has been written in the past 10 years about a phenomenon that develops among helping professionals and others known as *burnout stress syndrome* (Edelwich & Brodsky, 1980; Freudenberger & Richelson, 1980; Jones, 1981). Although definitions vary among these authors, burnout stress syndrome is perhaps best defined as "the identifiable clusters of feelings and behaviors most commonly found in stressful or highly frustrating work environments" (Paine, 1981, p. 6). According to Paine, the burnout syndrome, if full blown, can include a range of personal indicators such as health indicators (e.g., fatigue and chronic exhaustion), excessive behavior indicators (e.g., increased consumption of caffeine, tobacco, alcohol, or over-the-counter medications), emotional adjustment indicators (e.g., increased anger or tension, depression, or an inability to concentrate), relationship indicators (e.g., increased isolation from clients, responding to clients in a mechanical manner, or conversely, overinvolvement with clients—using clients to meet personal and social needs), attitude indicators (e.g., cynicism, boredom, or hypercriticalness of institution and/or peers), value indicators (e.g., sudden and often dramatic changes in one's values and beliefs). The burnout syndrome has been documented among a wide variety of helping professionals such as social welfare workers, physicians, psychiatrists, psychologists, police officers, psychiatric nurses, teachers, counselors, and ministers (Maslach & Solomon, 1980).

As a professional group, outplacement counselors have not experienced much full-blown burnout as yet. However, as helping professionals who experience many of the same stressors as do their counterparts, outplacement counselors need to be as mindful as possible, at the earliest point possible, of some of the initial ways in which the path to burnout can begin. Such early awareness makes possible early intervention. Early intervention can then act as prevention. For burnout, as for so many other symptoms, prevention is preferable to remediation.

What, then, are some of the early signals that outplacement counselors can identify that suggest that they might be on the path to burnout? One is a feeling of sameness: "I have already done this many times before." One colleague described it as feeling that "I have reviewed so many resumes at this point that they are all beginning to look and sound the same."

Another closely related symptom that counselors might experience is that of feeling like they are on automatic pilot, as if their approaches and interventions get trotted out in a rather mechanistic fashion. The counselor's interventions lack the freshness, vitality, and originality that suggest that the counselor is actively and creatively engaged with the clients.

Another symptom is that of feeling like a job search technician. Counselors begin to feel distant from clients, like there is not much of a genuine relationship. Rather, the outplacement work begins to feel like a process of tinkering with externalities, but not really connecting to the strongly held dreams, interests, values, skills, and ideas of the client. One colleague said "I feel less like a helping professional, which was my initial motivation for entering the field, and more like a functionary here to serve a steady stream of clients who view me a repairman." These are just a few of the many symptoms that practitioners might experience.

Outplacement Stressors

What then are some of the stressors or characteristics of the practice of outplacement that might contribute to the symptoms just described?

One way to examine the stressors of outplacement counseling is to view them as taking place at three different levels: individual/dyadic, organizational, and cultural.

Individual and Dyadic Stressors

Individual stressors are those that are located within an individual. They are person-centered stressors. For example, those drawn to outplacement counseling and other forms of counseling often take pride in their commitment to helping others. However, working closely with others on a constant basis is emotionally demanding. In order to avoid becoming overly stressed, practicing professionals must develop consistent methods of stress reduction that work for them. Some counselors might find this difficult to do. It might be because they do not recognize their own symptoms of stress, or it might be that they respond to their stresses in a manner that is nonadaptive or not healthy.

For example, one outplacement colleague always felt like she had to have the "right" answer in response to the questions and inquiries of her clients. Striving to always be right created a great deal of stress for her, and eventually contributed to her becoming much more defensive and threatened when clients asked challenging questions of her.

Another set of stressors are those that take place at the dyadic level. They emerge from the interactions of the counselor and client. Counselors have different styles and different sets of needs. The same is true for clients. Most experienced counselors know that there are certain types of clients who are more stressful than others for them. For example, one outplacement colleague places great importance on his role as a helping professional. He switched to outplacement from corporate human resources, where he did not feel like he had sufficient opportunity to be of genuine assistance to those he served. He worked very hard to accomplish the transition from human resource generalist to outplacement counselor. He thought he had arrived in a role where everyone would appreciate his genuine commitment to helping. Subsequently, he found it very stressful to work with help rejecting clients; those individuals who frequently had a "yes, but..." response for his interventions or who had a "yes, I will" response for him, but then never followed through with any of the ideas on which they, seemingly, had agreed.

Organizational Stressors

Another set of stressors are those that are organizational in nature. These stressors are related to the working conditions under which outplacement counselors operate. Some stressors are more common for those outplacement counselors who are members of a firm. Other stressors are more common for per diem counselors. For example, for those affiliated full time with a firm, stressors include:

- What are the expectations around the size of a caseload that the counselor carries?
- How manageable and realistic are the expectations?
- To what extent is there organizational support and recognition for feelings of overload?
- To what extent is there a culture that allows counselors to acknowledge openly that there are certain clients with whom they are struggling?
- Is such an acknowledgment met with collegial support and efforts at assistance, or is it responded to as if it reflects inadequacies and limitations on the part of the counselor?
- To what extent is there variety in the job for the counselor?
- Is there an opportunity for taking on special projects, or is there an unbroken string of one-to-one counseling sessions?

For per diem counselors, stressors include:

- How predictable are their assignments?
- How steady is their income stream?
- To what extent do they feel as valued and respected as the full-time counselors?
- To what extent do they feel in control of their career and its direction?

The answers to these questions can go a long way in determining the level of stress experienced by counselors.

Cultural Stressors

A final set of stressors are those that are cultural in nature. Outplacement services take place in a larger context, and are influenced by social, economic, and historical factors. Most counselors would agree that the average job search takes longer than it did several years ago. Right Associates, a leading national outplacement firm, has documented this trend. They found that in 1988 the average length for an executive job search campaign was 25 weeks. By 1993, the average length of a search campaign was 32.25 weeks, an increase of 29% (J. Aron, personal communication, February 1, 1994). Consequently, counselors work with clients for longer periods of time. Frustrations can build. Disappointments can mount. In addition, there are other marketplace factors that are stressful. Many candidates are constantly confronted by reports of job market "gloom and doom" and can become easily discouraged about future prospects. Other candidates are convinced that this will not be the last time in their careers that they will face job elimination. This, too, can be very disheartening. Further, many candidates are forced to take jobs at smaller organizations that they view as less prestigious than their former companies.

There does not appear to be any quick end in sight to the economic difficulties that have lead to so much downsizing in recent years. Marketplace instability is international in nature. It affects organizations in all industries. There are no safe havens to which clients can be directed. These conditions complicate the career planning and job search efforts of the candidate and can lead to great stress for candidates. They can easily have the same effect on counselors.

Remedies to Prevent Burnout

Given the many stressors that can impact outplacement counselors, it becomes very important that efforts are made to enhance professional growth and development. These efforts are the best insurance against counselor burnout and make it possible to increase the amount of satisfaction and gratification derived from the work.

There are three types of action: those that can change immediate counselor behavior, those that enable counselors to benefit from professional development opportunities, and those that enable counselors to benefit from career development opportunities.

Changing Immediate Behavior

In terms of changing immediate behavior, counselors can stop certain behaviors within the counseling relationship that are stressful, limiting, and emotionally draining. For example, counselors who are overly invested in being an expert at all times can pull back from that stance. They can strive to be more comfortable not having all the answers. They can do a better job of drawing on other resources, identifying other sources who can be of assistance to the client. Specifically, there might be professional colleagues who are more knowledgeable about information resources or industry information, to whom a client can be referred. Also, counselors can do a better job of regularly recharging their batteries. Each counselor will do this differently. For some it might be spending the lunch hour quietly, reading or reflecting. For others it might mean engaging in a more outer-directed activity (e.g., shopping, lunch with a friend).

Professional Development Opportunities

Another action that counselors can take is to seek professional development activities. These can take many forms. Supervision, seminars, and professional organization membership are very useful. So are taking classes, professional reading, and teaching.

Supervision is discussed more fully in chapter 13, as it has the potential to be the most important professional development activity. An effective supervisory experience, whether it be with a more senior counselor or a group of one's peers, can deepen significantly a practitioner's understanding of the counseling process and the nature of counselor–client interactions. It can also enable counselors to make a very thorough evaluation of their strengths and limitations and provide guidance in making necessary improvements.

There are a variety of seminars that can further professional development. For example, seminars that enhance counselor knowledge of assessment tools and techniques are frequently attended by outplacement practitioners. Involvement in professional associations such as the IAOP and the AOCF allows for stimulating professional exchanges. Some practitioners desire more intensive, full-length courses. Offerings in such areas as organizational psychology, cognitive/behavioral therapy, and management/leadership, among others, can be useful.

Reading broadly can certainly contribute to professional development. There are many topical areas that are relevant to the work of outplacement practitioners. Among them are future societal trends and directions, business news and current events, human resources practices, psychology, and counseling. Professional presentations are yet another vehicle for growth and development. Once again, the presentations can take a variety of forms. They can be one-time offerings to community or business groups, or full- length courses in continuing education or university settings. Writing articles for professional and academic journals or newsletters is another option that can contribute to professional development.

Career Development Opportunities

The third action that counselors can take is related to career development. Career development activities are certainly related to professional development activities. The major distinction is that although professional development activities aim to broaden counselors' outlooks and enhance their skills in the present, career development activities are those that counselors undertake with more of a long-range perspective about their career planning.

There are at least three paths of career development that have been identified (Bowers & Pickman, 1993). The first is to grow within the profession of outplacement counseling. The second is to expand beyond it. The third is to make a transition out of it.

In terms of growing within the profession, there are a number of activities that can be considered. Taking on more responsibility within one's current organization is a possibility. Counselors can identify needs that are not being met or projects that could be undertaken. They could also become more visible and active within the profession. The rapid expansion of the IAOP organization in the past several years has created many opportunities for practitioners to become involved in a professional organization at both the regional and/or national level. A third possibility for growth within the profession is to develop a niche of special interest and expertise. For example, one very well-regarded professional colleague has developed a full-time niche, specializing in working with outplaced individuals in job search teams.

A second approach to career development is to expand beyond outplacement counseling. With this approach, individuals develop practice areas that they pursue in addition to outplacement. In other words, for these individuals, most of whom are independent providers rather than full-time firm members, outplacement counseling is one of several areas of professional practice. In some cases, this approach is taken in response to financial necessity. In other cases, it is chosen to provide variety and a range of options. Among the additional areas in which outplacement professionals practice are organization consulting, diversity consulting, typology training, human resources consulting, and program development, especially career programs in not-for-profit settings.

A third option taken by some is to make a transition out of the practice of outplacement. Although the number of practitioners who have been in the field on a full-time basis for a substantial period of time, and who then choose to leave, is relatively small, there are some who have done it. They might leave to do related work within a corporate organization (e.g., to develop programs related to management training, leadership, internal mobility, and career development). Or, they might leave the field to pursue other unrelated interests, as did one colleague who became the chief administrator of a large church as a way of connecting more closely to her religious and social values. In general, however, because of the relative newness of outplacement, there is not much of a track record about what one does after a career in outplacement counseling.

In summary, outplacement counselors increasingly find themselves attending to issues of professional development. There are certain historical and sociological factors that contribute to this trend. Professional development is especially important for outplacement practitioners in order to prevent counselor burnout. There are a wide assortment of activities that promote professional development. In addition, there are a variety of approaches for promoting long-range career development among outplacement professionals. These activities and approaches are important to counteract the stresses of outplacement practice.

Chapter 13

Supervision

In chapter 12, "Professional Development," counselor supervision was described as one of the most important activities that can contribute to practitioner growth and development. This chapter looks more closely at the topic of supervision.

Rationale for Supervision

Supervision, in this context, can be defined as the process by which individual counselors discuss with fellow professionals and/or supervisors the clinical and/or job search issues raised in connection with the counseling services they provide.

Historically, business and counseling traditions differ around the issue of supervision. Those who have undergone formal counselor training typically receive supervision as a part of their program. This is true of those individuals whose background training is in psychiatry, psychology, social work, psychiatric nursing and counseling, among other fields. The rationale for the supervision is that counselors are called upon to be simultaneously both observer and participant in the counseling interaction, and that it is a very difficult challenge to enact well both of these roles. It requires a sophisticated understanding of the role of counselor as change agent. It also demands that counselors understand as fully as possible the impact of their behavior on others and the impact that others have on them. Such an understanding is best developed, according to counselor educators, when individual counselors are encouraged to examine their thoughts, feelings, and counseling behaviors in a nonthreatening setting with assistance from experienced practitioners and/or peers. Almost all counselor training programs require such training experiences, and recognize that without them counselor development is likely to be limited.

There is no comparable tradition of supervision in most business settings. Professional development in business settings is more likely to take one of two main forms. The first is training or skill enhancement offerings. The second is employee evaluations and/or feedback. Although opportunities for training and development are provided in many companies, these opportunities, by and large, tend to be of a didactic rather than experiential nature. Typically, they involve some form of classroom instruction. In general, individuals are not provided with the opportunity to review their work-related behaviors and feelings with well-trained supervisors and/or peers in a supportive atmosphere. Nor are they encouraged to self-disclose about the full range of reactions to their on-going work relationships. Those rare programs where individuals are asked to examine these matters tend to be of a more limited duration, rather than part of an on-going process.

Performance evaluations can also be used as a vehicle for professional development. In a well-conducted performance evaluation individuals receive constructive feedback that enables them to examine their work-related behaviors and establish plans for improvement. Most human resource professionals, however, would agree that the success of performance evaluations in contributing to professional development is mixed, at best. Far too many managers are not skillful in providing consistent and helpful feedback to their employees. So, for these reasons, most individuals whose background is in business have not been exposed to the same type of intensive, systematic, on-going supervisory experiences as those who come from a counseling tradition.

As discussed in an earlier chapter, some outplacement counselors come from corporate backgrounds, others come from counseling backgrounds. Clearly, there are relative strengths and weaknesses that counselors will bring to outplacement based on prior experience. Nevertheless, regardless of background, the complex nature of outplacement counseling demands that practitioners be committed to professional development on an on-going basis. Participation in supervision experiences is a prime method for enhancing professional development.

Most outplacement firms do not do all that they might on a systematic basis around the issue of counselor supervision. Often, it tends to be done on an informal, catch-as-catch-can basis. In those situations where it is more formalized, the focus tends to be on what can be referred to as *group problem solving* around specific client issues. The focus tends to be more on what can be done to change the client or the client's job search behaviors, rather than focusing on the contribution of the counselor to the counseling process. Although the former focus is useful and necessary, more attention also needs to be paid to the latter. Counselors need to be assisted and encouraged to deepen their understanding of the counseling process by examining both clients and themselves. The potential benefits of doing so are as follows:

1. Increased understanding. It can be liberating for counselors to articulate their thoughts and reactions about their counseling relationships. Feedback from other counselors can broaden their understanding.

2. Counselors can obtain specific ideas and suggestions from others. This makes it possible to bring fresh approaches to counseling relationships.
3. Counselors can see patterns in their counseling approaches more easily. By discussing their counseling relationships regularly, counselors are better able to perceive the way in which their typical approaches might be limited.
4. Counselors can learn from the modeling of their peers. So much of counseling is done behind closed doors. Open discussions with colleagues can provide a more concrete picture of "how others do it."
5. Trusting relationships with peers. Exposing one's work to others can result in increased trust and confidence in others. This can facilitate more frequent consultations with peers when problems arise.

Goals of Counselor Supervision

What are the goals of counselor supervision and how will practitioners know if they are developing and making progress toward these goals? Stoltenberg and Delworth (1988) described a model of counselor development that can be applied to outplacement practitioners. According to their model, counselors move through a sequence of stages as they develop from beginning counselors to advanced counselors. Each stage is characterized by certain behaviors and concerns on the part of counselors. Stoltenberg and Delworth pointed out that not all counselors at the same stage are exactly alike in every way. However, it would be a mistake to assume that no similarities exist among counselors at the same stage. Among the dimensions of counselor development examined by Stoltenberg and Delworth are intervention skills competence, client conceptualization, assessment techniques, and goal setting.

Beginning counselors tend to want training in circumscribed skills and look for specific structured formats to follow in implementing the skills. Their strong desire for structure often reflects a self-focus, rather than a client focus. The apprehensions and anxieties common to counselors at this stage cause them to focus on their own fears and uncertainties making it difficult to effectively empathize with or understand what the clients are experiencing. Counselors at this stage tend to think that they will find the "right" way to do things if they focus on their predetermined intervention strategies. They can be so focused on remembering how to use a counseling intervention that little attention is left for understanding the clients' perspective. This makes it difficult to respond effectively to unexpected or unplanned behaviors and statements by clients.

As for client conceptualization, beginning counselors often focus on specific aspects of clients' history, current situation, or personality style to the exclusion of other relevant information. Sweeping conclusions are often reached based on discrete pieces of information that fit consistently with the counselor's particular orientation, rather than their salience to the client's presenting situation. This hunt for consistency reflects the beginning counselor's wish for an uncomplicated and more manageable conception of the client.

In terms of assessment, beginning counselors are prone to overlook that test results, including those of supposedly objectively scored instruments, indicate merely the likelihood of certain vocational interests, personality styles, and cognitive styles, rather than the certainty of these attributes. The theoretical constructs underlying the tests are seen as primary, as counselors strive to fit clients into neatly defined categories. Counselors at this stage can easily focus more on their anxiety concerning the assessment situation, rather than the client's emotional concerns. Integration and interpretation of test results can seem "cookbook," with an effort to focus on consistency among results and an inclination to ignore discrepancies.

Finally, in terms of goal setting, beginning counselors often have difficulty in describing their goals for the counseling process. In addition, they have difficulty in visualizing the process of counseling and how they will assist the clients in getting from start to finish. Some beginning counselors are satisfied merely to get the clients to talk for most of the session, but are not yet able to devise a plan for dealing with the client's concerns.

How then do advanced counselors differ from beginners? Once again, the dimensions of intervention skills competence, client conceptualization, assessment techniques, and goal setting are examined.

In general terms, advanced counselors are more knowledgeable about themselves. They possess insight about both their strengths and their limitations, and are much less frightened and defensive about the limitations. They have confidence that they can grow and develop in the areas of weakness. Advanced counselors are better able to strike a balance between self-focus and client focus. They are able to focus intently on the client empathizing in the "here-and-now" moment. At other moments, they can pull back and process their own thoughts and feelings. They are able to flow smoothly back and forth between these two stances. The increased awareness of self and others characteristic of more advanced counselors enables them to gain access to important information from clients, as well as to access their own very important personal, emotional, and cognitive responses to clients.

More specifically, advanced counselors have a larger repertoire of counselor interventions available to them. They are also more skillful in the execution of their interventions. They are able to integrate these interventions with their client conceptualizations and counseling goals in a way that allows them to more confidently make rapid shifts and modify their interventions during the counseling sessions if a given intervention is not working effectively. Typically, they are also more creative and flexible in their use of interventions.

As for client conceptualization, more advanced counselors are better able to see clients more fully and richly with less of an inclination toward one dimensional thinking. Although models and general information are still valued, counselors at this stage are better at seeing each client as a unique individual. They are less prone to rely on stereotypes and less likely to pigeonhole clients on the basis of such factors as age, gender, or job function. Counselors at this stage are better able to see clients as both individuals and persons in context. They are better able to see how client variables such as age, gender, and job function interact to produce the whole person.

In terms of assessment, advanced counselors have developed a more solid handle on assessment techniques. They have developed clear preferences for certain instruments, and use them more skillfully. They are aware of both the value and the limitations of formal assessment instruments. Because they are less anxious about using the assessment tools, there is less self-focus and more ability to elicit client reactions, thoughts, and feelings in connection with test results. Finally, there is less of a need to focus on the consistency of results, and an increased ability to make productive use of discrepancies.

Finally, more advanced counselors are much better able to describe their goals for the counseling process and to visualize how they will assist clients in moving toward the goals. There is an increased ability to integrate assessment and conceptualization of the client with intervention strategies. Plans are more focused and coherent and can be appropriately altered as the situation warrants.

To this point, the discussion has focused on the importance of supervision as it impacts counselor development. Providing supervision can also be very important from the organizational perspective of managing an outplacement firm. One can make the case strongly that the major resource of outplacement firms is the experience and skill of their counselors. Therefore, providing for the systematic development of these counselors is an important consideration in the success of the firms. A well-conceived and skillfully executed supervision program can help in attracting, retaining, and developing top-notch counselors. It enables practitioners to remain motivated and enthusiastic about their work, as they feel that they are developing their skills as professional counselors. Their motivation and enthusiasm can spread to other employees of the outplacement firm, thereby enhancing organizational morale.

In summary, the outplacement counseling process is a complex one. It requires the counselor to be both participant and observer of the process. Counselors need to understand the impact of their behavior on others and the impact that others have on them. Supervision, as practiced in programs of counselor education, is a proven and effective way to promote this type of professional development. Supervision can also be very useful in developing outplacement counselors from beginner to advanced stages of functioning. Some form of supervision is increasingly important if outplacement practitioners want to continue improving as counselors. Also, providing supervision can enhance the outplacement firm's organizational morale. Outplacement practitioners need to consider how supervision models can be formulated that will suit their special needs and allow for on-going professional development.

Chapter 14

Cross-Cultural Issues

Cross-cultural issues in outplacement counseling are the focus of this chapter, which also addresses some of the demographic and industry trends that make cross-cultural issues more timely.

Work Place Diversity

The composition of the U.S. workforce is changing very rapidly. In 1987, the Hudson Institute released an influential study, *Workforce 2000*, which was done for the U.S. Department of Labor. The study concluded that the overall U.S. workforce would increase from 124.7 million in 1990 to 150.7 million in 2005. Of the 26 million new workers, 85% would be women, immigrants, and/or members of minority groups (Williams, 1992). In short, the workforce is becoming, and will continue to become, increasingly diverse. Learning to manage this diversity will become a major challenge for business and industry leaders.

Although only a few years ago the idea of diversity in the work place was being dismissed as a fuzzy-headed notion with little relation to production or process, the idea is now being taken seriously. More and more employers are devoting company time and money to cultivating diversity and learning to manage it effectively. They acknowledge that they need to recognize, respect, and capitalize on the different racial and ethnic backgrounds of U.S. society. They see diversity as good business, as well as good public relations. They hope that managing diversity well will result in fewer costly discrimination suits, and a more tolerant and innovative workforce that will be in a better position to generate new ideas and to solve problems in creative ways. If these are not reason enough, employers are gradually coming to recognize that the future of the United States in a global economy will rest with individuals who understand cultural differences and can function across racial, ethnic, cultural, and linguistic lines (Williams, 1992).

90

Counseling Implications of Diversity

What then are the implications of these trends for outplacement counseling? First, to the extent that the workforce becomes more diverse, those individuals receiving outplacement services will also become more diverse. In the early days of outplacement a very large percentage of the clients were middle-aged White males with senior management positions. That has changed in recent years, and is likely to continue changing in the future. It will change because the workforce is becoming more diverse. It will also change because outplacement services, either group or individual, are no longer offered only to senior executives. Increasingly, they are offered to middle and lower level employees too.

With a more culturally diverse population to serve, outplacement practitioners will need to improve their understanding of cross-cultural issues. According to Derald Wing Sue, a recognized expert on cross-cultural counseling and therapy, counselors need to work toward three objectives in dealing with culturally diverse clients (Wakelee-Lynch, 1989).

First, counselors need to become more aware of their own values, biases, and assumptions about human behavior. This means becoming more aware of the stereotypes, racial attitudes, and beliefs that they have about other groups.

Second, counselors need to try to understand the different world views held by culturally diverse clients. Various ethnic groups experience the world differently, and this has an impact on group members' values and beliefs. The following are just some of the various dimensions around which cultural groups differ:

- notions of self,
- use of communication and language,
- standards concerning dress and appearance,
- practices around time and time consciousness,
- attitudes about work habits and practices,
- views about relationships,
- mental processes and learning styles, and
- norms about physical space and space relations (M. A. Lee, personal communication, July 7, 1993).

With so many important dimensions along which people can differ, it becomes especially important for counselors to recognize that their world view, values, and beliefs might not be the same as those of their clients. Understanding more about how culture has influenced the values and beliefs of their clients, as well as themselves, will allow counselors to understand their clients more fully.

The third aim, according to Sue, is for counselors to develop intervention strategies that are appropriate for the lifestyle and world view of the various ethnic and racial groups from which their clients come. Counselors will need to be more skillful at selecting culturally appropriate intervention strategies that reflect the understanding that different cultural groups might require different approaches.

At the same time that he argued for increased understanding of cultural differences, Sue cautioned against overgeneralizing based on cultural assumptions. There is heterogeneity within groups as well as across groups. Individual differences must be recognized. Counselors must avoid the temptation to apply a single intervention strategy to all individuals within any group.

At this point, it is useful to examine a few specific situations where cultural issues might impact on the career-related behavior that is the focus of outplacement counseling. These examples are in no way exhaustive, but, hopefully, they provide some very concrete situations in which cultural factors are manifested in career issues.

Susan Rhee, a counselor who works extensively with Korean Americans, pointed out that Koreans might not make the best impression in interviews because they are taught to focus on good listening skills rather than on verbalization skills (Backover, 1991). In addition, emphasis is placed on hierarchical relationships that involve subordination and respect for authority. Consequently, in interview situations that involve an authority figure, Korean Americans might be more hesitant to assert themselves or ask questions for fear of appearing impolite. The interviewer could easily mistake the relative silence or brief responses as a lack of self-confidence or ability. Further, she pointed out that Koreans are socialized to speak indirectly as opposed to directly. If asked by an authority figure about his or her ability to do a job, a Korean American might provide an answer that sounds noncommittal or unenthusiastic, when in fact, he or she does believe him or herself to be very well qualified.

Most outplacement counselors coach clients to maintain eye contact in interviews. This, too, might prove problematic for those whose cultural norms maintain that looking directly into the eyes of another is a mark of disrespect, rather than an expression of confidence and sincerity, as mainstream U.S. culture suggests.

Understanding cultural differences is important for outplacement counselors and clients, not only at the interview stage, but also around more general issues of career management. M. Lee (1990), an expert on career counseling with Chinese Americans, pointed out that Asians are hard to find at upper levels of management in corporate America. Although overt prejudice might be a contributing factor, Lee maintained that often an unfamiliarity with the subtleties of career management, based on cultural differences, can also limit career advancement. For example, many Chinese Americans do not understand the importance of visibility in successful career management. Or, if they do at least understand its importance, they might balk at seeking it. Seeking visibility runs counter to the culturally valued traits of humility and group achievement. Instead, Chinese Americans might assume that hard work and excellent performance reviews will ensure promotions, and, therefore, are both confused and upset when these approaches do not earn the desired results.

Understanding cultural differences around issues of career management is very important in working with African-American clients as well. African-American executives receiving outplacement services often report having had to confront many day-to-day challenges while managing their careers in corporate America. Although these challenges might not always have been obvious to their Caucasian colleagues, they were experienced as all too real by the clients. The situations can take many forms. Some of them are quite subtle; others less so. Among the more common are an apparent disregard for an assigned task by a subordinate, a lack of urgency in completing an assignment, and the neglect of comments made during a meeting.

Other African-American clients report always feeling like they have to prove themselves. Alean C. Saunders, an organizational consultant for diversity programming at Kaiser Permanente Medical Care Programs in Oakland, California who holds a doctorate in education, articulated the feeling. "I feel like I'm always proving myself. Getting people to think that I have anything to say that is worthwhile and that I have the credentials to do what I do is a constant challenge..." (Byrd, 1993, p. 27). Still other clients report that they are sometimes not seen as team players because they lack interest in the kind of after hours socializing that is routinely expected of executives in their corporation. Outplacement counselors need to be aware of these situational dynamics in order to provide maximum help to their African-American clients around the full range of complex career management issues they face.

In summary, the U.S. workforce will continue to become increasingly diverse. As a reflection of this situation, outplacement clients will become a more diverse group as well. In order to achieve the best results, outplacement practitioners will have to become culturally skilled counselors. This means having the awareness, knowledge, and skills to intervene effectively in the careers of clients from culturally diverse backgrounds. Culturally skilled counselors face many challenges. They need to be able to view each client as a unique individual while at the same time taking into consideration the common developmental experiences that all people face, as well as the specific experiences that come from the client's particular cultural background. Beyond this, counselors need to be constantly aware of how their own cultural experiences have shaped them as individuals and as professionals (C. Lee & Richardson, 1991). It is the combination of awareness, knowledge, and skills that will enable outplacement practitioners to work most effectively with the increasingly pluralistic and diverse workforce of the future.

Chapter 15

Women and Outplacement

Do men and women have similar experiences in outplacement? If not, in what ways are their experiences different? This chapter focuses on these and related issues. The discussion is divided in two sections. The first looks at the experience of women as outplacement clients. The second examines the experience of women as outplacement counselors.

Female Outplacement Clients

As in so many other areas of outplacement practice, there is very little systematic data gathering that has been published around issues of women in outplacement. One of the few studies comes from the Southern California office of a national outplacement firm, Lee Hecht Harrison. The authors, Phelps and Mason (1991) made the following conclusions:

1. The distinctive needs of women managers and executives drive a different outplacement process.
2. Women often take longer than men to go through their transition, staying in outplacement 38% longer.
3. Gender bias still exists.
4. Women tend to approach outplacement from a perspective that perplexes their male colleagues, the men in their personal lives, and even their male counselors.
5. Older women may opt out of the corporate track altogether, excited by the prospect of blazing more rewarding trails as entrepreneurs or consultants.

Approximately 64 executives took part in the study that covered a 2-year period. Of the executives, 18 were women. As a group they were older than their male counterparts. More than half were single; the number of those earning high salaries was only slightly lower than for men.

It is entirely possible that the data in this study are not generally representative of the experience of women in outplacement. Freeman and Haring-Hidore (1988), for example, suggested that there are important differences between women in high-skilled jobs and women in low-skilled, hourly wage jobs. They contend that these differences warrant some tailoring of typical outplacement services to better meet the needs of women in low-skilled jobs.

However, rather than focus on the possible methodological limitations of the Phelps and Mason study, it is more useful to use it as a jumping off point for discussion about some of the issues for women in outplacement.

One issue is whether women experience job loss differently than their male counterparts. One line of thought is that for men, more so than for women, a sense of self becomes increasingly associated with the job; the organization; and the salary, power, and perks they provide. Therefore, job loss propels men into an all-out race to find a new job as quickly as possible in order to replace what has been lost. Men down play the emotional aspects of losing a job. They see job loss as an unfortunate event that needs to be fixed. They attribute the job loss to external conditions such as marketplace forces or organizational politics, rather than their own limitations or inadequacies. Therefore, they may take the rejection of job loss less personally. Also, they are more likely to separate or compartmentalize the job search from other aspects of their life.

Women, on the other hand, according to this line of thought, are seen as culturally conditioned to have their identity more closely linked to having satisfying relationships, including the relationships with work associates. Therefore, job loss results in a disruption of important relationships. It is not merely a matter of substituting one source of income for another, for much of what has been lost is interpersonal in nature.

A second area concerns the extent to which women are able to compartmentalize the job loss experience. Women are culturally conditioned to fulfill a number of roles simultaneously—wives, mothers, daughters, and workers. Consequently, women are called upon to integrate work, partnership, children, household, and community on an on-going basis. A change in one area affects all the others. When job loss occurs, it cannot be compartmentalized easily. The job loss threatens to upset the complicated balance of these various domains.

Women might seek different sources of support in the face of job loss, especially compared to more senior male executives. The traditional male executive is married and more often than not his wife does not hold a paying job outside the home. This was true of 87 newly promoted male executives in a study by Farrell in the mid-1980s and reported by Phelps and Mason. In such cases, the traditional marriage can be both a source of support and a stressor in the face of job loss. On the one hand, a male executive might have a partner who has been a loyal source of support throughout the development of his career, and continues to be so following job loss. On the other hand, the nonemployed spouse of a male executive might exert considerable pressure on him to get out and find another job, because so much of her identity and status is linked to his career success. Her feelings of both economic and social vulnerability might lead to an increased sense of urgency that then impacts on her husband in his job search efforts. These feelings can be intensified if she is unable or unwilling to get a job herself.

This situation is likely to change with the increase in dual-career couples. Job loss will influence the dynamics of such couples differently than those of single-career couples. Anecdotal reports suggest that it is already doing so. For example, although a male executive who has lost his job might not experience the loss as quite so onerous if his spouse is employed outside the home, she might find it very stressful to have all the financial responsibilities shifted to her shoulders. Or, a female executive who has lost her job might use the situation to reconsider the work–family balance of the household. She and her partner might decide that she will look for part-time, rather than full-time, employment in order to devote additional time to childrearing responsibilities. Although job loss is still likely to be a stressful event for dual-career couples, they might have a broader range of potential responses for dealing with it.

How does the situation differ when a high-level woman loses a job? First, the family situation and support level might be different for the female executive than for her male counterpart. A higher percentage of executive women are either divorced or never married. A Korn–Ferry International study cited by Phelps and Mason determined that 45% of executive women are single. So, they might never have had the on-going support of a spouse to assist in career building. In terms of financial pressures, on the one hand, female executives might be less likely to have a spouse pressuring them to go out and find a job quickly. On the other hand, if female executives are unmarried and solely responsible for their own financial support, then the economic pressures are no less significant than those of males in the same circumstances.

Historically, female executives were not as likely to have an extensive network of professional support at the highest executive levels. Male executives have more of a tradition of mentorship and coaching. There is a more long-standing pattern of having opportunities opened up to them by well-placed others. Female executives, on the other hand, typically received much less counseling and mentoring along the way. A less-developed network exists to help them advance in corporate circles. So, in a number of different ways an outplaced female executive might feel less supported in her career than her male counterpart.

For this reason, Phelps and Mason (1991) contended that it is especially important that the outplacement process provide intensive and consistent support that takes into account the special needs of female executives. Among their recommendations is finding a counselor who is a good match for the candidate. Specifically, they underscore the importance of having outplacement counselors, at least some of whom are women, who work hard to empower women. They also stress the need for counselors who are skilled in entrepreneurial options as many women are exploring businesses of their own, consulting practices, and smaller entrepreneurial firms as alternatives to large corporations. Finally, they recommend establishing on-going women's discussion groups in the outplacement firm offices as a vehicle for providing support, acknowledgment, candor and feedback.

On the other hand, S. Spanier (personal communication, September 9, 1993) questioned the practice in outplacement firms of separating female clients for special treatment such as segregated discussion groups. Although this practice might provide additional psychological support, it can also isolate the females in much the same way that they have been set apart, historically, in corporations. They might miss out on the opportunity for interactions with male outplacement clients that produce collegial and coaching relations. Further, according to Spanier, male outplacement candidates could also benefit from the special services earmarked for women. Male clients are just as likely to be struggling in response to job loss as their female counterparts.

Female Outplacement Counselors

This section focuses on the experience of women as outplacement counselors. Once again there is little systematically gathered data on the topic. Gallagher (1990) surveyed approximately 300 outplacement practitioners and provided some interesting demographic information about outplacement practitioners. A high percentage of his respondents (27%) were firm owners. Of his respondents, 25% were women. Among the major findings were the following:

1. Female practitioners were younger than male counselors. Their average age was 41.9 compared to 50.1 for males.

2. Female practitioners had fewer years of business experience. Their average number of years in business was 15.8 compared to 25.2 for males.

3. Female practitioners had fewer years of practice in outplacement. Their average experience was 5 years compared to 6.4 for males.

4. Female practitioners were much less likely to be in ownership positions. There were 12 female owners compared to 66 male owners.

5. Female practitioners were equally well educated as their male counterparts. The same percentage of females and males reported having a master's degree. The same percentage of females and males reported having a doctorate degree. It does appear, however, that there are gender differences in the type of studies reported as majors. At the bachelor's level more than three times as many males as females majored in business. At the master's level nearly twice as many males majored in business. At the doctoral level nearly four times as many males concentrated on business. On the other hand, female practitioners were much more likely to have majored, at the bachelor's level, in the social sciences (psychology, sociology, political science), education, or liberal arts. At the master's level, more than twice as many females concentrated in one of these areas. At the doctoral level, approximately three times as many females concentrated in these areas.

6. Female practitioners were equal to male practitioners in their number of careers prior to outplacement. Each group averaged approximately three prior careers. However, there were some notable differences in the nature of their former employers. Females reported approximately twice as often having worked principally in the field of education. They were also engaged significantly more often in working for government, not-for-profit, or religious organizations. Male practitioners reported twice as often having worked principally for publicly held corporations, predominantly Fortune 100 companies.

7. Female practitioners earned significantly less money than male practitioners. Female practitioners, on the average, earned approximately $48,000, whereas male practitioners averaged approximately $83,000. This large difference appears to be at least partially attributable to the large discrepancy in compensation between owners and nonowners. The compensation of owners is nearly double that of nonowners, and, as was previously noted, males were more than five times as likely as females to be firm owners in the Gallagher study.

What conclusions can be drawn from this data about the involvement of women as outplacement counselors? First, females practicing outplacement counseling are much less likely to be at the ownership level than their male counterparts. Females are equally well-educated as their male counterparts although their education is more likely to be in the social sciences, education, or liberal arts than business. Their prior experience is less likely to have been in large publicly held corporations than in government or the not-for-profit sector. Their compensation level is well below that of their male colleagues, attributable at least in part to the discrepancy in income between owners and nonowners.

Although the Gallagher data seem fairly consistent with my more impressionistic observations, it is possible that the proportion of female practitioners is higher than the Gallagher data suggest. However, it still seems that the female practitioners are disproportionately represented among per diem or freelance consultants, rather than among those counselors employed full time at outplacement firms. The data certainly suggest that the outplacement industry is one in which opportunities for women exist. The extent of those opportunities and the status of women in the industry deserves much additional examination and discussion.

In summary, the experiences of females in outplacement have been examined in order to determine how they compare with those of males. Attention has been focused on both female candidates and female outplacement counselors. Few studies have been conducted concerning gender differences in outplacement. The data that are available suggest that there are certain areas of similarity, but other areas where gender differences exist.

Chapter 16

Family Issues

As discussed in earlier chapters, the effect of job loss can be highly stressful for individuals whose positions have been terminated. The terminated employees, however, are not the only ones who are affected. Their family members are impacted as well. Job loss has repercussions throughout a family system, and can produce a wide range of reactions among family members. This chapter examines some of those family reactions and the ways in which outplacement services have responded to these issues.

Spouse and Job Loss

Probably the most common way in which outplacement practitioners acknowledge the impact of job loss on families is in their willingness to meet with the spouse of a terminated employee. Most outplacement firms have had some firsthand experience in allowing candidates to bring their spouses to one or more of the early meetings with the outplacement counselor. Such a meeting typically includes the counselor, candidate, and spouse. The purpose of the meeting is often to educate the spouse to the outplacement process and to identify ways in which the spouse can be helpful to the candidate throughout the job search. Such a meeting is especially important if the spouse is unfamiliar with the outplacement process and/or has some mistaken assumptions about it.

For example, Leonard B. was a candidate who was quite unfamiliar with networking concepts and practices at the outset of outplacement. He trusted his counselor's advice to refrain from immediately calling his every contact to inform them that his job was eliminated and to ask them if they knew of any available jobs. Alternatively, in the first few weeks at the outplacement center Leonard and his counselor worked on developing a marketing-oriented resume, improving his interview techniques, and developing effective networking techniques. Nevertheless, Leonard reported to his counselor, in these early days, that his wife was very concerned and quite critical of his search efforts. She did not understand how he was going to find a job without asking people directly if they had one. Leonard was not able to explain networking principles to her satisfaction. The counselor invited Leonard's wife to a joint session and provided an overview of the outplacement process and a rationale for the way in which Leonard was proceeding. His spouse left the meeting with a more complete understanding of the outplacement process and was, reportedly, far less critical as the search unfolded.

Other outplacement practitioners recognize that, even if a family responds well to the initial days of job loss, issues can emerge as the job search process unfolds. Therefore, family issues can be addressed at later points in the process, as well as at the outset. The counselor might choose to work directly only with the candidate around some of these issues on the premise that the candidate can, in turn, act to improve the family situation. Or, alternatively, the spouse might be invited to the outplacement offices for some consultation sessions. According to Harding (1991), a whole host of different family issues can emerge. The following are among the most common.

What does a family say to other people about the job loss? In general, it is best to provide full details judiciously, perhaps only to intimate friends and/or family. For most others it is best to provide a brief, generally positive and forward looking statement.

Usually, the tone of the family's reaction will be set by the terminated employee, and other family members will take their cues from that individual. For example, if the terminated individual initiates candid, open, and nondefensive discussions, it can assist other members in dealing with their emotions in similar fashion. In other situations, however, spouses can respond even more intensely than the terminated individual, especially if the spouses have been invested heavily in the career success and status of their partner. Kathy Bourne, who originated the spouse consulting program at Jannotta Bray & Associates, a Chicago-based national outplacement firm, said that "spouses often express more anger and stay mad longer than the person who loses a job." The anger will usually be directed at the former company or boss (Harding, 1991).

Another set of issues concerns family finances. Once again candid discussions will help. They allow for the development of some clear expectations. It is important that these discussions go beyond general assurances that "everything is going to be fine" or general warnings that "we'll all have to tighten our belts a little." There might need to be changes in spending patterns. Less money might be available to meet basic requirements of food, clothing, and shelter. Or, less money might be available for leisure and recreational activities. The more specific the discussions, the less likely that there will be mixed signals resulting in over or under budgeting. The assistance of a professional financial advisor can bring some objectivity to this often very emotional issue. Some outplacement firms provide access to such professionals.

The disruption of established family patterns is another set of issues that can emerge. The job seeker might be spending more time at home. This could cause strain on the spouse who was accustomed to his or her own domestic routines and does not welcome having to make adjustments or modifications. Or, a spouse who had not previously been employed outside the home might need to take a job. Resentment or ill will could ensue. On the other hand, for some family members the change in patterns might be very welcome. An unemployed parent who is spending more time at home will, undoubtedly, have the opportunity to spend more time with children. Parent–children bonds can be strengthened. Or, although a certain spouse might resent having to take a job outside the home as a result of job loss, another spouse might view it as a welcome change or an opportunity for personal growth and development.

Another set of issues that might emerge revolve around relocation. A job seeker might have to consider relocation in order to secure a desirable position. Clearly, this step would have implications for other family members. For the spouse it could mean starting a new life without the built-in contacts that the job would provide for his or her newly employed partner, or that a new school would provide for children. In some cases, there might be a history of multiple relocations in response to corporate reassignments. A spouse might be less willing than in the earlier years to undertake another such relocation.

Children and Job Loss

To this point, the primary focus has been on how a spouse might be affected by job loss. Children, however, are also very much influenced by such a family event. Their possible concerns and reactions warrant some specific comments.

Children will respond differently to job loss in the family depending on their ages and developmental stages. Younger children might need to be reassured that their parents can still provide a stable and secure world for them. Older children probably have a more realistic understanding of the situation, but might still have fears in connection to it.

Children will likely have reactions to some of the same issues raised by Harding (1991). Children need information in connection with job loss that is appropriate to their ages. This will help them adjust better themselves and will also help them communicate to others about the family situation. Harding described the pride he felt in his 5-year-old son when one of the boy's friends asked in surprise, "You mean your dad's not working?" While everyone waited for the young boy's response, he recalled how he had been coached by his dad. He replied confidently, "No, but he's looking for work."

Children certainly are impacted by the finances of job loss. A variety of family activities and decisions might have to be altered. For a young child it might mean fewer holiday or birthday presents. For other children it might mean foregoing summer camp or private lessons of a favorite activity. For older children it might mean changes in those colleges that are viable. A professional colleague who works as an admissions counselor at a local community college described the pain and anger that sometimes emerged in her office. During one family meeting, the mother, unemployed father, and daughter, a high school senior, were sitting quietly listening to the admissions counselor extol the virtues of her institution. Suddenly, without warning, the daughter turned to her father and screamed "This is all *your* fault. If you hadn't lost your job I could still go to Sarah Lawrence [a prestigious private college with high tuition] with all of my friends."

Children certainly are impacted if a job search results in relocation. Kathy Bourne and Faye Woocher, of Jannotta Bray, advised candidates to avoid discussing this issue with children until it is clear that it will happen. They have seen teenagers who flatly declare that they will not move away from their familiar friends and schools. In many cases, the teenagers are responding most strongly to the perceived loss of control in their lives. However, if all the information is then presented in an appropriately forthcoming manner, including both the specific attractions of the new situation as well as the substantial losses associated with the old situation, there is a better chance that a teenager's stance can be relaxed.

Dumas (1992) provided some guidelines about how to talk with children about job loss. First, she encouraged parents to level with their children. Children depend on their parents for truth, and can sense when something is weighing heavily on their parents. Keeping children in the dark makes it possible for them to conjure up far worse scenarios than need be. The amount of detail provided will depend on the age and maturity of the child.

Next, she warned against creating a false sense of reality. Some parents, for example, shower their children with new treats or toys in an effort to shield them from the stresses of job loss. This can create a false sense of reality that is confusing for children. They know that their parents are concerned about finances, and, yet, new presents are being purchased. The children might begin to question their own ability to understand reality. Or, they might question the truthfulness of their parents.

Further, Dumas encouraged parents to let the children help out. A child can be made to feel like a valued member of the family if asked to contribute and resolve problems in an appropriate way. Dr. Antoinette Saunders, founder of the Chicago-based "The Capable Kid" counseling centers, has some specific suggestions. For example, a family chart can be constructed on which each child lists how he or she has been helpful in a given week. A 4- or 5-year-old might list "played quietly by myself while Daddy was on the phone" or "brushed teeth by myself while Mommy was writing letters." A 7-year-old might have contributed by "helping to clear the table every night," whereas an 11-year-old might have "helped get the baby ready for bed so Dad could send out more resumes." The caution here is that parents must find the right balance by letting the children help out but not overburdening them with responsibilities that are inappropriate. Optimally, children can be informed about important family developments, encouraged to contribute to possible solutions, but, at the same time, not be made to feel responsible for fixing the situation. Saunders recommends the holding of family meetings as a way of finding this delicate balance. The family meetings provide an opportunity for everyone to speak and to share (Dumas, 1992).

Spouse Counseling

To this point, we have focused on the more common practice of inviting the spouse of an outplacement candidate to join counselor and candidate for one or more sessions. In this model, even though the reactions of the spouse are elicited and valued, the focus remains on the candidate. The spouse's involvement is very much in the service of the candidate.

There is another, more progressive, model. It provides for a more extensive counseling relationship with the spouse. Specifically, it provides a dedicated counselor who establishes an on-going, confidential relationship with the spouse, which is separate and apart from the relationship between the outplacement counselor and outplacement candidate. Janotta Bray is an industry leader in this regard, and has a very fully developed program of this type (J. L. O'Day & F. Woocher, personal communication, April 2, 1993).

This model is designed to provide support and consultation to the spouse throughout the job search process. The goals of this relationship are to provide: (a) education to the spouse about the outplacement process and (b) on-going counseling around those job loss-related issues that impact on family functioning. The articulation of these goals is not dramatically different from the more common, less extensive model. The significant difference seems to be in the manner in which the goals are implemented. Having a separate, but equally confidential relationship with a different counselor provides spouses with a clear message that their concerns are significant and are to be respected. It also implies that the spouse's concerns might not be identical to those of the job-terminated partner, but, nevertheless, deserve attention from a trained professional.

According to O'Day and Woocher, a wide range of issues can emerge in working with spouses. In some cases the focus is more directly on the career issues of the spouse. For example, some spouses might choose, or be compelled, to seek paid employment outside the home in response to their partner's job loss. The spouse might not have had much job search and/or career planning experience, thereby necessitating considerable work with the counselor.

In other situations, the focus might be on how the spouse can assist and support the job-terminated partner. Efforts are made to identify and review very specific behaviors, because in some cases the spouses feel they are behaving in a manner that is helpful, but the outplaced partners do not experience the behaviors as helpful. For example, in one situation the spouse thought it would be helpful for her husband if their home was free of noisy distractions when he returned there at the end of the day. Accordingly, she saw to it that their children were either visiting friends or engaged in quiet activities when their father came home. For his part, he was spending his days at the outplacement center contending with the anxieties and uncertainties of job search. He felt like the normal rhythm of his life had been seriously disrupted. He relished the thought of returning at the end of the day to the customary hustle and bustle of his home. It was a way for him to feel reconnected to his loved ones and heartened that there was continuity, at least in his domestic life. The spouse's counselor helped her to see that, despite her good intentions, she had not arrived at the best solution. She was encouraged to keep the family routines as close to normal as possible in order to be truly helpful to her partner.

Increasingly, attention is paid to dual career issues. For dual-career families a job loss can easily disrupt the typical patterns of how various responsibilities and sacrifices are distributed. For example, when one job is lost, the partner who is still employed would likely feel more responsibility for the family's financial well-being. In turn, he or she might expect the unemployed spouse to pick up more of the domestic responsibilities. However, this can easily become a conflict for unemployed spouses who feel that all of their time and energy needs to be spent searching for a job. Job loss often turns out to be a time when couples are confronted with some of the underlying expectations and implicit contracts they have with one another. Harding maintains that solutions to issues like these need to be based on mutual respect for the respective contributions of each family member. Differences in compensation or time commitment will exist. Yet, both careers need to be acknowledged for their importance and their value to the family system. Specific solutions will vary depending on the individual circumstances, but effective communication and mutual consideration are critical.

In summary, job loss has repercussions throughout the family system. Issues emerge that might necessitate changes in family patterns. These adjustments are often stressful. However, the experience can have its positive aspects as well. As with all crises, the opportunity for growth and development presents itself. Important family lessons can be learned. Children can learn that by pulling together in difficult times a family can negotiate very bumpy roads. Adults can gain insights about their families and themselves. The family can emerge stronger and more cohesive after living through a job loss. Skilled outplacement counselors can play a very important role in assisting families in responding to the challenges of job loss.

Chapter 17

International Issues

Outplacement counseling was initially developed in the United States in the 1960s and 1970s. It has since spread rather impressively to other parts of the world. Currently, Canada has a very well-developed outplacement industry. Professional outplacement services are provided in at least 14 European countries and 6 Latin American countries. There is also an outplacement industry in Australia as well as in certain Asian countries. This chapter provides information about the outplacement activities in these international areas. It identifies some key issues and compares and contrasts the international practice of outplacement with its U.S. counterpart.

Outplacement in Latin/South America

Outplacement services are provided in six Latin American countries: Argentina, Brazil, Chile, Paraguay, Uruguay, and Venezuela. Each country has its own culture and style and these differences influence the manner in which the outplacement industry operates. At the same time there are similarities across the various countries of the region.

First, it is useful to look briefly at some of the demographics of the region. Latin/South America has a combined population of approximately 300 million, that represents about 5% of the world's population. There are approximately 106 million people in the workforce, approximately 31% of whom are female. Average unemployment is 7%. Average annual income is approximately $2,100 per year (U.S.). These statistics certainly suggest that this area is a substantial market in an increasingly globalized economy (Mejías, 1993).

In terms of outplacement activity, some general trends can be noted. Outplacement was introduced into this region in the 1980s. Companies providing outplacement services are, in general, also offering other human resources services such as recruiting and compensation consulting. Approximately 80% of the activity is corporate, where a sponsoring organization provides services for its outplaced individuals. The other 20% of the business is retail, paid for by the individual. Average fees for corporate business are 15% of annual compensation; average retail fees are $2,500 (U.S.).

The average client is a male between 40 and 50 years old, as only 3% of management positions in the region are held by females. The candidate is likely to have had approximately 10 years of service in his organization, and is typically a university graduate.

The scope of outplacement activity in the region is still relatively modest. The number of organizations providing outplacement, including branches of leading international firms such as Drake Beam Morin and Right Associates is less than 25. The number of outplacement professionals is less than 60. The typical sponsoring organizations who purchase outplacement services are branch operations of U.S. companies, banks, large and mid-sized family-owned industrial companies, and large national companies. In addition, there are those individuals who purchase retail services.

In comparing outplacement practices in Latin/South America with those of the United States, several features are notable. First, strong labor laws have a direct bearing on the outplacement industry. In Argentina, for example, companies are required by law to provide very generous severance in the case of job eliminations. Specifically, a company must provide at least 36 months of salary equivalency for an executive who has had 3 or more years of service in a given company. Although this situation is slowly beginning to change, it clearly makes the marketing of outplacement services difficult if their cost is added to already expensive, mandated severance payments.

In terms of the emphasis of the outplacement program in Latin/South America, there appears to be a strong focus on educating clients about the labor market and on providing very specific advice and guidance about it. The outplacement professionals are in the habit of working very closely with executive search firms and company human resources directors in order to provide candidates with very specific job development leads.

Finally, in a development that seems similar to that of the United States, there is a growing trend toward entrepreneurial alternatives for displaced workers, as opportunities within the historically large employers are not as readily available as in the past.

Europe

Outplacement services are provided in 13 European countries: Austria, Belgium, Denmark, Finland, France, Germany, Ireland, Italy, Netherlands, Norway, Spain, Switzerland, and the United Kingdom. As in Latin/South America, there are different cultures and styles that have an impact on the manner in which outplacement is developing in the various countries. There are also some similarities across the European countries whose total population is approximately 360 million.

In terms of outplacement activity, the European countries can be roughly divided into the following three groups based on the level of maturity that outplacement has thus far attained: highly developed markets (Belgium, France, Netherlands, and the United Kingdom), developing markets (Denmark, Finland, Germany, Ireland, Italy, Norway, Spain, Sweden, and Switzerland), and undeveloped markets (Austria, Greece, and Portugal; Murray, 1993).

The United Kingdom is the largest market thus far with annual revenues at approximately $100 million. The Netherlands is a market where a large percentage, approximately 30%, of those whose jobs are eliminated are provided with outplacement services. Germany has the potential to be the strongest and most influential market in Europe given its population of 80 million people. Thus far, however, outplacement has developed rather slowly in Germany.

In terms of more general trends, the outplacement industry in European countries appears to pass through several stages of maturation. Initially, there is a period of educating business executives about the scope and nature of outplacement activities. This is followed by a period of growth and expansion. The next phase is one in which the marketplace becomes more saturated and, therefore, more highly competitive. In the third phase, outplacement firms try to establish favorable market segments and niches, and both sponsoring organizations and individual candidates become more knowledgeable and, often, more demanding consumers. One of the manifestations of this increased competitiveness is price cutting and programmatic adjustments. Fees are often reduced for nonsenior clients, time limited services are offered, as are volume discounts. The reduction of fees for nonsenior clients highlights an outplacement practice that some European firms follow that their North American counterparts do not. Certain European firms charge a higher fee for older clients. The rationale is that these clients will be harder to place because of their age, and, therefore, the outplacement firm is entitled to a larger fee.

As with their Latin/South American counterparts many of the European outplacement professionals are very proactive about job development on behalf of their individual candidates. They work closely with search firms and personnel directors to generate market intelligence across industries and job disciplines in order to advise candidates on the specific skills required in rapidly changing marketplaces.

Another trend among European outplacement professionals is the growing number of cross boundary linkages. Practitioners in Europe have already been active in joining professional organizations such as the IAOP. Through this affiliation they have been able to establish relationships with colleagues in other countries, thereby facilitating professional exchanges and potential cross-border referrals. This trend will likely continue as the European countries move toward an increasingly regionalized political and economic structure.

Another issue that has emerged in several European markets is that of taxation of outplacement services. As in the United States and Canada, government officials in several European countries have raised the issue of whether outplacement services should be treated as a taxable benefit to employees. Thus far, the issue has been resolved in the United Kingdom with a ruling that outplacement is not a taxable benefit. In France, the issue is still unresolved. In some of the less developed markets the issue has not as yet been addressed.

The taxation issue raises the larger question of the extent to which government and regulatory bodies will take action that impacts on the outplacement industry. On this issue there seems to be some differences across the European countries. Certain of them, especially Spain, Italy, and to a somewhat lesser extent, France, have a history of more extensive government and bureaucratic involvement in labor markets. In these countries government has traditionally played a bigger role in any situation involving large-scale layoffs. Therefore, these governments might be more inclined to consider regulating those elements, such as outplacement services, that are linked to such large-scale reductions in force.

In summary, outplacement counseling has spread from its roots in the United States to a host of countries on several continents. On the one hand, each country has its own business culture and style that has a distinctive impact on the way in which outplacement services are developed and delivered. On the other hand, certain trends and themes appear consistently across different countries and regions and have an impact on the practice of outplacement across the world.

Chapter 18

Ethics

Like most new industries, outplacement counseling has grappled in its formative stages with issues of maintaining quality and standards. One result of these deliberations has been the formulation of a code of ethics by the Association of Outplacement Consulting Firms (AOCF), the professional organization of outplacement firms. In addition, more recently the AOCF has developed a casebook that deals with some of the specific situations around which ethical dilemmas are likely to emerge, and provides recommended guidelines for dealing with such situations.

The IAOP, the professional group organized by individual practitioners, has also been active around issues of ethics. It has very recently formulated a document of standards for ethical practice, which is designed to address those issues most relevant to individual practitioners.

This section identifies some of the specific ethical issues that emerge most often in outplacement practice. Space limitations prevent a full discussion of the guidelines for responses to such situations, but brief recommendations are provided. The reader can refer to Axmith (1991), the AOCF Casebook on Ethics and Standards for the Practice of Corporate Outplacement (1991), or the International Association of Outplacement Professionals Standards for Ethical Practice (1993) for further information.

Ethical Issues and Delivery of Counseling Services

One of the characteristics of the outplacement industry that complicates issues of ethical practice is the dual client relationship that exists. The outplacement counselor is paid by the referring corporate sponsor and, yet, provides services to the individual client. Inevitably, this poses conflicting interests. Determining the proper way to manage these conflicting interests has been the thrust of much of the work in the area of ethics.

Progress Reporting

One set of issues revolves around progress reporting. Typically, the outplacement practitioner is asked to report to the sponsoring organization on the progress of the individuals being sponsored. On the one hand are the interests of the corporate client. Its representatives want to be informed about the services being provided to the candidate, the candidate's status and progress, and any possible barriers to progress. In general, the company representatives are looking to be reassured that the candidate is in good hands and that their resources are being well spent. On the other hand, outplacement practitioners want to inspire trust in their candidates, and usually do so by ensuring confidentiality about all material presented in session. This is very important to candidates because they might be revealing personal and sensitive information about themselves to the counselor during sessions. The information might also concern individuals and situations in the sponsoring organizations. In either case, it is likely that candidates would not want such information transmitted to the sponsoring organization.

Does progress reporting, written and/or verbal, to the corporate client about candidates represent a violation of confidentiality? If not, how should the information be reported? To date, the ethical norms that have emerged recommend that feedback to the corporate client should be general and give an overview of client activities and progress, rather than specific and detailed information. References to such information as the candidate's assessment results and lists of contacts are generally omitted. The situation becomes even murkier in those cases where the candidate is making little progress. In such cases the outplacement firm might not be eager to report limited progress out of concern that it will reflect poorly on the firm and the quality of the services it provides. In other cases, the candidate's lack of progress is attributable to some highly personal problem such as a divorce or substance abuse. In all these cases the firm and its counselors must decide to what extent, and in what way, confidentiality can be balanced with customer accountability.

Other issues around reporting can emerge. For example, how should a counselor respond in a situation where the candidate requests that the counselor not inform the sponsoring organization that the candidate has secured a new position? The candidate wants his or her bridging payments to continue, and knows that if his or her new position is reported the payments will stop. In this case a widely accepted guideline is that the counselor is obliged to report to the corporate client when the candidate has secured a new position. Other firms handle the situation somewhat differently. They are willing to have the counselor report merely that the candidate has discontinued use of the services and prefers that his or her whereabouts not be made public. The firm's practice around this issue should be made clear to the candidate at the outset.

Or, how should a counselor respond if the candidate's behavior suggests he or she might be a threat to self or others? The counselor is concerned that if he or she shares this information in order to prevent a disaster from occurring, confidentiality with the candidate is breached. In this case, immediate consultation with a qualified professional, usually a physician or psychologist, is recommended for the outplacement practitioner. Beyond this, the practitioner is obliged to inform a third party who might be at risk. The practitioner also has an obligation to inform appropriate third parties (family members, physicians) who might be able to intervene and prevent the candidate from harming him or herself or others.

There are related issues that pose a less serious threat. There are instances, for example, when a candidate is referred for outplacement counseling, but the practitioners reach the conclusion that the candidate is suffering from some psychological or medical problems that will prohibit effective use of the services. The recommended course of action is that the corporate sponsor be informed about the situation, so that more appropriate services, such as those of the employee assistance program, can be provided.

Within these general guidelines both individual counselors and outplacement firms vary in terms of how they handle the issue of confidentiality. Specifically, there are some counselors who, even while acknowledging their dual allegiance to both sponsoring organization and individual candidate, align themselves more closely with the candidate. They are very careful not to report highly specific information. Other counselors feel a stronger allegiance toward the sponsoring organization and are willing to be more liberal in disclosing specific candidate information. Sometimes, the reporting is done through a third-party account manager rather than directly by the counselor in order to free the counselor from this dilemma. Similarly, some outplacement firms have very clearly articulated practice guidelines around these issues, whereas others do not. In most cases, clear policy guidelines can greatly facilitate the effective management of these matters.

Litigation

Another set of issues emerges around the topic of litigation. If a candidate threatens or initiates litigation against the corporate client, a number of complicated issues can emerge. First, if the candidate asks the counselor whether a "fair" settlement has been provided by the employer, how should the counselor respond? Counselors need to remain mindful of the dual relationship with sponsoring organization and individual candidate, and state this clearly to the candidate. Depending on the response of the counselors, they could easily be seen as being in a conflict of interest by one or both of the parties. Therefore, it is very important that outplacement practitioners not be in the position of giving legal advice.

A related situation can occur if the candidate does decide to bring a lawsuit against the corporation. What should the counselor's stance be? Should counselors attempt to persuade the candidate not to do it? Once again, counselors who actively try to dissuade a client from initiating a suit could be seen as being in a conflict of interest, and providing advice beyond their area of expertise. Yet, counselors need not stand idly by. They can certainly help the candidate understand the full consequences of pursuing such a course of action, including the possible impact on the candidate's job search and future career development. Beyond helping the candidate in this way, some outplacement firms consider it their obligation to inform the sponsoring organization that the candidate has sought legal advice. In such a case, the practitioner would need to determine the best way to inform the company in general terms without violating the client's confidentiality.

Other Issues

Another set of issues emerges around the relation between outplacement and executive coaching. Sometimes an outplacement firm is called upon by a sponsoring organization to assist one of its employees whose career might be stalled, or where the job fit is problematic, or where a reassignment is under consideration.

One potential dilemma is that the outplacement firm might be seen as having an investment in seeing to it that the candidate eventually leaves the organization. This could result in a second assignment, in this case an outplacement one, for the same firm. In effect, this would be a type of double dipping. Recommended guidelines are that the outplacement firm make an offer at the outset to remove itself from consideration as the outplacement firm of record if the candidate eventually decides to leave the sponsoring organization. This offer removes the perception of narrow self-interest. Or, more frequently, the outplacement firm will deduct its fee for executive coaching, its first assignment, from the outplacement counseling fee, its second assignment.

A second situation in this area is one in which the sponsoring organization uses the executive coaching program to oust the employee in a "back door" fashion. In effect, the decision has already been made to outplace the individual. The executive coaching is a pretense. In such a case the counselor is advised to not take on such an assignment. Rather, he or she should inform the corporation to act on its predetermined decision to outplace, rather than subject the employee to a misleading, manipulative exercise.

Another ethical issue that can emerge concerns the proper approach for dealing with important information that is known to the counselor but not to the candidate. Specifically, suppose the following situation. A candidate is in the final series of interviews for a position in one of her targeted companies. The position would be a step up for the candidate who is, therefore, very excited at the prospects. However, the counselor is aware that the manager in the target company to whom the candidate would report has been accused several times in recent years of sexual harassment of his direct reports. The counselor was told of these accusations while working on a prior assignment for the same target company. How should the counselor proceed? Should he provide the candidate with information learned on a prior corporate assignment? Should he tell the candidate what he has heard about the manager or do nothing? In such a case it is recommended that the counselor put the candidate in touch with others who can provide a realistic picture of the hiring manager.

Another delicate ethical issue that can arise is that of a sexual attraction between candidate and counselor. What is the outplacement counselor's ethically proper response to a candidate who declares a sexual attraction for him or her? In this type of situation counselors must always maintain respect for the candidate's welfare and focus the outplacement activities toward a positive resolution for the candidate. The very strongly recommended course of action, therefore, is to refrain from any romantic involvement with the client. Further, if the counselor is no longer able to work effectively with the candidate as a result of the situation, arrangements for transfer to another counselor should be made.

Ethical Issues and Marketing

Thus far, the ethical issues raised for discussion have focused on the delivery of counseling services. Ethical issues exist around the marketing of outplacement services as well. In general, they fall in the category of making promises that cannot be kept. For example, what if prospective candidates are informed during the exploratory or shopping meeting that they will be working closely with firm owners or principals? In practice, the owners or principals see the candidates for the first session or two before transferring candidates to less senior consultants. How should such a situation be handled? Candidates should be clearly informed during the exploratory meeting about the amount of time they can realistically expect to spend with the owners or principals, and also be informed about and meet those consultants with whom they will spend the bulk of their time.

A second issue related to the ethics of marketing concerns efforts by the firm to strongly suggest that there is a job waiting for candidates if they sign up with them. In these cases the firm suggests to candidates that they have corporate clients who could use someone with the candidate's qualifications. The implication is that there are real, concrete job prospects known to the firm. In reality, the firm is merely speculating about possible job prospects or might have a database of positions which are not necessarily appropriate for the client. How should such a situation be handled? During exploratory meetings, firms should not make reference to specific job prospects for a particular candidate unless there is a concrete, justifiable basis for doing so. To do otherwise is to take unfair advantage of candidates' need for hope and their wish to resolve their career situation instantly and effortlessly. Further, if the candidate perceives the outplacement counselor as a placement professional, it can change the nature of the counselor–client relationship. For example, the candidate might present him or herself exclusively in a "selling" mode, like he or she would to an interviewer or an executive recruiter. This could short circuit the more collaborative, frank discussions that are central to the outplacement counseling relationship.

There is another common issue concerning the marketing of outplacement services. In their marketing and promotional efforts, outplacement firms might be asked by potential clients to provide information about former clients that attests to the quality of the services delivered. In responding to such requests, outplacement counselors are strongly advised to receive permission in advance from the sponsoring organization or individual candidates prior to passing along their names as references. To do otherwise is to breach confidentiality. In a similar vein, if a practitioner refers to individual candidates in a written article or public speech, fictitious names should be used and care must be taken to ensure that the identity of the candidates cannot be discerned from the description.

Although the examples given here are not exhaustive, they do provide an indication of the type of ethical dilemmas that can easily emerge in outplacement practice and the type of guidelines that have been recommended.

The IAOP, although less than 5 years old, has also devised a set of standards for ethical practice. It provides detailed guidelines around a number of areas including consulting relationships with corporations, consulting relationships with individuals, professional practice, and business development practice. In addition, it has a rather lengthy section on guidelines for conducting assessment and testing of individual candidates. Although there is considerable overlap with the AOCF guidelines around general principles, there is a marked emphasis in the IAOP standards on practicing within the limits of one's competence and adhering to established professional practices. This is most clear in the section on assessment. In addition, there is an emphasis on promoting ethical behavior toward candidates, including demonstrating respect for the candidate at all times, maintaining confidentiality of the counselor–client relationship, promoting the welfare of the candidate, and encouraging and assisting the candidate to take responsibility for decisions during the employment transition.

In summary, the field of outplacement has begun the ongoing process of addressing issues of ethical practice. General ethical standards have been formulated by both of the major professional organizations. Guidelines around specific ethical dilemmas that emerge regularly in outplacement practice are recommended. Materials that have been prepared by the professional associations can be consulted for more detailed information.

Chapter 19

Relation of Outplacement to Other Career Development Professionals

Outplacement, as it has been discussed throughout this book, is a service sponsored by an organization for its employees whose jobs have been eliminated or terminated. The services of the outplacement organization are paid for by the sponsoring organization, not the individual candidates. Outplacement practitioners are not the only professionals, however, who provide career-related services.

In fact, the rapid pace of change taking place in today's work environment has resulted in an increase in the number of individuals and organizations seeking professional assistance in connection with career-related concerns. This chapter examines two other groups of professionals who provide career-related services. It compares and contrasts their services with those of outplacement practitioners. The two groups are individual career counselors in private practice, sometimes referred to as retail counselors, and organizational career development consultants.

Growth of Demand for Career Services

Before looking more closely at the work of individual career counselors and organizational development consultants, a few general comments are in order. First, there seems to be a strong need for the services provided by career development professionals. A 1990 Gallup poll, National Survey of Working America, commissioned by the National Career Development Association, underscores the extent to which Americans need help in planning and managing their careers. About 44% of employed adults were either unsure about the future of their jobs, or definitely expected to leave their current employer by choice or forced termination within a year. Sixty-five percent indicated that if they could plan their work lives again, they would definitely get more information about job options. Only 40% indicated that they had planned their careers (National Career Development Association, 1990).

However, it might be premature for career development professionals to draw overly optimistic conclusions about the demand for their services. The bad news is that most people do not seek professional help in connection with their careers. Of those polled, 42% went to friends or relatives, 10% did not know where to turn, and 9% did not seek any assistance. Seeking professional help for their career is an option that most individuals do not choose.

Career development professionals can have different titles, outplacement consultant, career counselor, organizational career development consultant, to name a few. The circumstances under which they provide services can differ, as can the focus of their interventions. What they essentially have in common, however, is their efforts to facilitate the best possible match between individuals and the work that they do.

Individual Career Counselors

I begin with a look at individual career counselors. According to Sywak (1992), most of those clients who eventually work with career counselors have made an effort to actively seek out the counselors. Typically, this is done in response to a level of distress or confusion related to the individual's career or job. Payment is provided by the individual, who is usually looking for some advice, guidance, or information.

The training and background of career counselors is difficult to define systematically. So is the number of professionals who practice it. No accreditation or licensing is required. A small number of individuals have gone through a national licensing process. According to the National Board of Certified Counselors, only 938 individuals have fulfilled the requirements to be a national certified career counselor. They tend to be grouped in several large states—14% in California, 10% in New York, and 9% in Texas. In practice, the way things currently stand, anyone can call him or herself a career counselor and go into business. Private practitioners have background training in a variety of disciplines. There is no one background route to the work. Many practitioners have a master's degree in counseling or a related area. Others have a background in corporate human resources or in the helping services.

In terms of the focus of their services, career counselors can cover a wide range. Services might include self-assessment including testing, occupational exploration, and decision making. Some counselors also assist clients in the development and implementation of a marketing and job search strategy. Others do not, and focus only on the career assessment and planning.

Launching and sustaining a career counseling practice is not an easy task from a business point of view. As acknowledged earlier, although there might be a general need for career services, there is not a widespread clear understanding of what career counselors can do for clients. Some clients have unrealistic expectations. In the extreme, their fantasy is that in a matter of a few sessions the counselor will give them a quick fix. The counselor and his or her bag of tests will tell them what occupations are right for them. The answer will lead them effortlessly to an enjoyable and profitable new career. For such clients, some up-front time needs to be spent in creating realistic expectations.

Another difficulty in establishing a private practice is translating the generalized need for assistance into a steady stream of paying clients. Unlike other forms of counseling, which often require a longer period of treatment, career counseling is typically of limited duration, most often fewer than 10 sessions. Client turnover is high. Also, there are very few sources of third-party payment as there are for other counseling services. Consequently, the paradox presents itself that, even though there appears to be a great need for career services for a large number of people, few counselors, relatively speaking, are able to make their living as full-time independent career counselors.

For those who are engaged in successful private career counseling practices, fees range from $40 to $125 per hour. Some counselors price their services on a session-to-session basis. Others offer their services in a package that includes additional fees for testing.

Sywak (1992) noted several characteristics of those who build successful private practices. Some have had a successful professional career in another field and use the credibility from it, as well as their former colleagues, to build a base of referrals. Some start with a sharply focused specialty—lawyers, corporate executives, re-entry women—and then branch out.

The most successful practitioners appear to be energetic, persistent, and effective in their networking. They market themselves effectively. This can be done through a variety of activities. Teaching adult education classes, addressing community groups, writing articles for local newspapers, and developing strong referral networks with other professionals—executive recruiters, therapists, teachers, corporate human resource officers are among the most common. Being simultaneously involved in a variety of professional activities appears to be a very common phenomenon for individual career counselors. Sywak labeled it a *composite career*. For example, they might do some contract or consulting work for an outplacement firm, have some private practice clients, and do some teaching. For some counselors this multiple role career is a matter of financial necessity. For others, it is chosen as a way to provide variety, breadth of experience, and intellectual enrichment. Those not interested in managing the business aspects of a private practice, with its requisite marketing demands, might seek employment as independent contractors for nonprofit career centers or agencies that provide career-related services.

Organizational Career Development Consultants

Next, I look at organizational career development consultants. Some of this work is being done by the same organizations and individuals who provide outplacement counseling, whereas some of it is being done by others who are not involved in outplacement.

As their rate of growth has slowed in the past few years, and as profit margins have shrunk, outplacement firms are raising questions about their long-term prospects. A number of them believe that growth will come from diversifying. Some have already developed practices that address various areas of human resources consulting including management development, executive assessment and coaching, organizational change management, and diversity management. The outplacement firms see this as a strategic business decision in order to remain competitive.

Others view this trend not just in strategic business terms, but as a logical extension of their expertise. Gallagher (cited in Sywak, 1992) compared it to

> the resident doctor in an emergency ward who sooner or later begins to champion gun control. You can't stay in this business too long before you want to get involved in prevention. You want to move upstream in an organization and work on the issue of matching people and jobs and developing people in their careers. Over the years we have been giving away lots of consulting in trying to get at the reasons why terminations happen. (p. 300)

Gallagher and others see the organizational career development work as a way to introduce more sophisticated career services prior to the point that jobs are eliminated.

While outplacement practitioners sort out their potential involvement in these areas, other career development professionals are also working on them, both internally and as external consultants. Sywak described three kinds of career-related work being done in organizations—individual counseling, training, and human resources systems development.

Individual Counseling. This type of counseling involves a key individual meeting with a counselor around important career issues. The sessions could address such issues as developing additional managerial skills, overcoming interpersonal limitations, or clarifying career goals, to name just a few. The goal is to assist the individuals in improving their performance, sharpening their focus, identifying suitable opportunities in the organization, or coming to the realization that leaving the organization is in order. In some situations the counseling is done by existing human resources staff. Other times it is done by outside consultants who are seen as providing greater assurances of confidentiality, a key component, especially for internal counseling programs where concerns about exposure can run high. This internal counseling process is referred to by a variety of names including inplacement counseling, executive coaching and management development.

Training. Training enables employees to update skills, acquire new capabilities, and enrich their current jobs. Training can be offered to a wide variety of target groups around a range of specific needs and/or problems. For example, an organization might choose to offer an internal career planning workshop to a group of employees whose jobs have been affected by a corporate reorganization and who, therefore, need to find new positions within the organization. Such employees might need updated skills in order to respond to changing technologies. Or, a workshop might be offered to a group of high potential employees in order to assist them in identifying the type of developmental assignments that would prepare them for senior management positions. Or, training might be offered to plateaued employees faced with limited promotional opportunities. Such training might enable them to find enrichment opportunities within their current position or identify new directions.

Many organizations recognize, in principle, that in order to attract, retain, and develop desirable employees they need to provide opportunities for growth and development within the organization. However, according to Leibowitz, Farren, and Kaye (1986), leading organizational development consultants, organizations typically do not effectively link their training offerings to employee needs and plans and/or organizational plans. Rather, they tend to offer training on a reward basis, such as attending a seminar or conference, a nuts-and-bolts basis such as acquiring skills needed only for immediate tasks, or on a smorgasbord basis, where the employees are left to make their own choices from a miscellany of offerings. Leibowitz et al. argued that in order to be maximally effective, training and development opportunities need to be more closely coordinated with employee and organizational needs.

Human Resources Systems. The third area of internal career-related work subsumes career counseling and training under the broader umbrella of comprehensive human resources systems. According to Sywak (1992), there is a growing movement among progressive corporations toward the development of more integrated career management systems and away from one-time-only, stand-alone career counseling and training interventions. Career professionals are being asked to link individual "career development concerns with strategic human resource planning and development by integrating human resource planning, performance appraisal, succession planning and management and executive development systems" (p. 301).

Career professionals are being asked to design career development systems that involve responsibilities for employees, managers, and organizations. Employees are asked to take responsibility for identifying their skills, values, and interests. They are urged to discuss their expectations with managers and seek information about appropriate options. Managers, for their part, are expected to support the career planning of their employees by providing clear and timely feedback around performance evaluations, discuss the formal and informal politics of the organization, provide opportunities for their employees to be visible, and link their employees to key resources and individuals. Organizations, for their part, are expected to make available important information about company mission, policies, and future directions. They also need to provide information on current options and possibilities, and support both employees and managers in their career development efforts through suitable training, education, and development opportunities (Leibowitz et al., 1986).

The professionals who consult successfully in this area typically have a background in organizational development and/or human resources systems, with a firm knowledge of performance appraisal, succession planning, human resource planning, and management and executive development. The Human Resource Planning Society is a professional base for many of those who are interested in this type of systems work. Although there are only a small number of individuals who are equipped to bring such a broad background to organizational career development consulting, those who perform it find it challenging and dynamic.

Comparisons Among the Various Career Professionals

How, then, does the work of the individual career counselor and the organizational career development consultant compare to that of the outplacement counselor? There are a number of dimensions along which comparisons could be made. Four are discussed here: background and training, clientele, level and nature of intervention, and future issues.

Along all four dimensions there are both similarities and differences among the various career development professionals. In terms of background and training, all three groups have low barriers to entry. Most of the well-regarded practicing professionals in the fields do have substantial experience in either counseling and the helping professions, or in business and industry, or in both domains. However, anyone can present him or herself as a career counselor, outplacement counselor, or organizational career development consultant. This raises complex issues of defining, regulating, and licensing the practice of these types of work. For example, how do these fields assure ethical and high quality service? Is it done via credentialing and licensing, or is it done via some other means? How do these fields communicate clearly about themselves to the public and to potential clients? How do they enhance the skill and expertise of their practitioners? These are open questions with which all the fields need to contend.

How do the fields compare in terms of their clientele? One major difference is in the source and sponsorship of the services. Career counselors receive payment directly from individuals who are seeking assistance in connection with career-related confusion or uncertainty. Counseling is typically of a more limited duration, attributable, at least in many cases, to the costs that the clients must bear. On the other hand, clients come from a very wide variety of occupations and settings, both traditional and nontraditional. Counselors, therefore, can find substantial challenges in working with very diverse clients.

Outplacement practitioners and organizational career development consultants, on the other hand, are paid by the sponsoring organization. Assignments often turn out to be of longer duration, making possible different types of counseling relationships. The individuals with whom the professional is working are members of a corporate organization. This has implications for the range of diversity to which the practitioner is exposed. The outplacement professional or the organizational development consultant is not as likely to have the opportunity to work with those who are employed in the full range of occupations (e.g., artists, athletes, helping professionals, civil servants, re-entry women, independent entrepreneurs, students, etc.).

The third dimension is the level and nature of the interventions. In this case, the career counselor and outplacement counselor have more in common with one another, and differ from the organizational career development consultant. Both the career counselor and the outplacement counselor typically work with individuals and/or small groups. Their focus is on facilitating change by informing, educating, and empowering individuals. The organizational career development consultant has a different focus and looks to promote change by intervening at a different level. For these professionals, the emphasis is placed on altering large-scale systems, not just specified individuals. Their efforts are directed at placing individual career development concerns under the umbrella of systemwide strategic human resources planning and development that is, in turn, closely linked to overall business strategy.

A fourth dimension is that of the future issues that these career development professionals face. One issue that all three groups face is whether the demand for their services will continue to grow. On the optimistic side, some suggest that the baby boom generation will see to it that the use of career development services continues to grow. The baby boomers are a large group who are more accustomed than previous generations to using mental health and counseling services, in general, and who have had more exposure to career-related services from their college career centers. Therefore, the thinking goes, they will either seek out career services independently, and/or insist that their companies provide some help around these matters, especially as both companies and individuals navigate the uncertain career waters in the years ahead.

On the pessimistic side are those who think that individual career-related services will only become widely used if third-party reimbursement payments become available for them. This development is not very likely, given the pressures on both government and employers to curtail health benefit costs. Also on the pessimistic side are those who think that the use of organizational development consulting services will not grow substantially. The rationale is that it will not grow because senior corporate managers remain unconvinced that the introduction of more comprehensive, sophisticated human resources systems impacts favorably on the bottom line. Further, the thinking goes, the human resources function remains undervalued compared to other functional areas of the corporation. Therefore, the commitment to improving it does not run that deeply.

In summary, the rapid pace of change in today's work place has resulted in an increase in the number of individuals and organizations seeking professional assistance in connection with career-related concerns. The assistance is provided by at least three different groups of professionals—individual career counselors in private practice, organizational career development consultants, and outplacement counselors. The services provided by these professionals have much in common; they also have some clear differences. All these professionals have an important role to play. Their expertise will be needed to assist both individuals and organizations in managing effective transitions in the face of rapidly changing employment conditions.

Chapter 20

Marketing Outplacement Services

The point has been made several times that outplacement counseling is a hybrid of business and counseling. There are a number of ways in which the juxtaposition of these two traditions manifests itself. Most of the chapters in this book have focused on counseling-related considerations. This chapter focuses on a topic that is clearly a part of the business aspect of outplacement—the marketing of outplacement services.

There are many different marketing approaches. The approach of choice in a given situation will depend on the product or service being marketed. Outplacement marketing is very much in the tradition of relationship selling. Cathcart (1990) defined *relationship selling* as a process where there is a "focus on building a good relationship with someone and providing a valuable service through that relationship" (p. 1). This chapter uses a model of relationship selling to discuss the marketing of outplacement services. Among the topics addressed here are the philosophy of the marketing approach, establishment and maintenance of the marketing relationship as well as some special considerations.

Traditional Selling Versus Relationship Selling

The traditional selling approach, especially for tangible goods and products, was viewed as a contest in which there was a winner and a loser. An act of persuasion was required where the seller talked the buyer into buying. It rested on the assumption that buyers must be sold, because otherwise they would not buy on their own. There was a major emphasis on the close of the sale. Great sellers were seen as highly persuasive individuals who could accomplish the close. A dogged determination was seen as valuable in getting the close. Other elements of the traditional selling approach included a one-sided sales pitch that did not vary much from client to client. Qualities valued in the salesperson were aggressiveness, competitiveness, and a thick skin.

Relationship selling contrasts with this approach in a number of ways. First, relationship selling is service-oriented. It is guided by an approach that can enable both buyer and seller to emerge as winners. It is seen as an effort to help the client rather than persuade the client. It is characterized by a cooperative approach to problem solving. Buyer and seller are viewed as partners, not adversaries. Communication is two-sided and is individually tailored to the specific buyer. The most important part of the sale is not the close, but the follow-through when the buyers receive the product or service they purchased. The master salesperson is not necessarily the one who is most aggressive and competitive, nor the greatest showman. Rather, the master salesperson is one who cares about the client. The master salesperson is also someone who is skillful at questioning the buyer to determine needs, and skillful in listening to the buyer's responses. In addition, an accomplished salesperson is highly perceptive about situational nuances. This refers to the ability to understand fully the client's business needs and to generate ready alternatives for effective intervention.

The marketing of outplacement services is very much in the tradition of relationship selling. Outplacement marketers are typically interested in establishing an ongoing dialogue with individuals in the sponsoring organization, building good relationships with them, and in providing a valuable service through those relationships. This approach allows for the establishment of trust between marketer and client. Creating and strengthening the trust is seen by the marketer as a critical element in receiving ongoing outplacement assignments from the sponsoring organization.

Outplacement Marketing Approaches

Outplacement marketers use a variety of promotional approaches. Certain of the larger and nationally known firms can rely more on advertising, written materials, public relations, and educational seminars to develop new business. Their reputation and industry visibility enhance the likelihood that such approaches will be successful. In addition, they look to establish links with professional firms in such fields as law, accounting, and executive search in order to generate leads or identify targets who might be interested in outplacement services. The larger firms combine these approaches with proactive personal selling. Smaller outplacement firms, those sometimes referred to as boutique shops, combine both sets of approaches as well. However, they are often less likely to rely on written promotional materials. Instead, they put the bulk of their effort on proactive personal selling.

Marketing outplacement services typically follows one of two patterns. In some outplacement firms there are dedicated marketers who focus exclusively on marketing the firm's services. They are not involved in providing direct counseling services.

In other organizations the professional staff functions in two roles, as both marketers and counselors in varying proportions. In this model, the professionals are expected to generate new business even as they provide on-going counseling services. There are advantages and disadvantages to both approaches.

For dedicated marketers there is the opportunity to develop greater expertise and sophistication about the function because they are devoting 100% of their time to it. Also, because they have chosen marketing as their professional specialization, they might be better suited to it. Further, the potential for conflict between the two roles is reduced. For example, individual candidates do not have to worry that their counselor is unavailable for an urgent consultation because the counselor is out of the office conducting a lengthy marketing call. Or, suppose the situation of a sponsoring organization that wants to register its dissatisfaction with the outplacement services one of its former employees is receiving. It might be harder to register their reactions if the same individual is both the account representative and the individual counselor who is the object of the dissatisfaction.

For those in the combined marketer/counselor role there is the opportunity to understand very fully the services being provided. In marketing the services the practitioners certainly know "from whence they speak," and can communicate the full flavor of outplacement counseling. Second, the combined role provides the opportunity for practitioners to engage in a wide variety of professional activities leading to the acquisition of a wide range of skills. Having such a multifaceted position is very important for some individuals.

In approaching sponsoring organizations, outplacement marketers find it very important to gain access to those individuals who have the responsibility for decision making about outplacement services. In the early days of outplacement, marketing was often done president to president, the president/owner of the outplacement firm to the president or chairman of the sponsoring organization. In recent years, as outplacement has become more widespread and better understood, the responsibilities have been delegated. Presently, in many organizations vice presidents or senior vice presidents in human resources make decisions about the selection of outplacement firms. In some situations the decisions are made by human resources professionals below the vice-presidential level.

An initial meeting is arranged where the marketer introduces the outplacement firm and its services to the sponsoring organization. The salient features of the firm are stressed as a way of distinguishing the firm from its competitors. Among elements that might be stressed are the quality and experience of the counseling staff, the commitment to customer service and follow-through, the proven track record of having successfully counseled executives in a wide variety of circumstances, the convenience of the firm's location, and the quality of the administrative support and value-added services such as computer-assisted research capabilities or job development activities. National firms might emphasize their ability to service the client's needs in whatever part of the U.S. or overseas markets that the need arises. Smaller firms might emphasize the amount of individual attention from firm principals or owners that an individual might receive. Smaller firms in different parts of the country have also banded together in affiliations that allow them to respond to the geographically dispersed needs of their clients. The member firms remain separate entities but make referrals to one another. The Lincolnshire Group and Outplacement International are two examples of such associations.

Price is also an important issue around which firms compete. Throughout the 1970s and into the mid-1980s the industry standard for full individual outplacement services was 15% of the client's total annual compensation that might include the client's annual bonus. Certain firms charged an additional administration charge in the $500–$1,000 range, others did not. Some firms charged a somewhat higher fee for senior executives for whom the most comprehensive services were provided including such features as a private office.

In the last few years, in the face of stiffened competition, some firms have chosen to reduce their fees to gain competitive advantage. It is often the larger firms with a higher volume of clients who are best positioned to reduce their fees. Those who choose not to reduce fees try to stress the benefits of their organization, thereby minimizing the price difference. They also try to increase the prospect's desire for their services, rather than arguing about the price. Pressure to reduce fees has also increased from sponsoring organizations, some of whom are no longer as able or willing to spend as much on outplacement services as in the past.

A successful sale of outplacement services is seldom accomplished at the first meeting. The initial meeting is more likely seen as the first step in the creation of an ongoing relationship. Follow-up is critical for the outplacement marketer, as multiple contacts are likely to be required before a sale is consummated. The follow-up can take many forms including phone calls, letters and cards, and subsequent meetings. Efforts are made to emphasize those portions of the sales approach that are particularly salient or meaningful for the particular individual being approached. Outplacement marketers vary in the extent to which they are customer-oriented. Some have a tradition of offering more or less standard products and services from which the customer can choose. Increasingly, however, efforts have been made to determine accurately the needs of specific clients and to develop more individualized and tailored services accordingly.

Once the sale is completed the most effective marketers turn appropriate attention to servicing the account. Consistent contact with the sponsoring organization is made. One of the major vehicles for doing so is the status or progress report on those individuals receiving services. The typical status report strives to strike the delicate balance of providing general information to the sponsoring organization about the individual for whom they are incurring the expense of outplacement, while at the same time preserving the confidential nature of the counselor–candidate relationship. Providing consistent and useful feedback to the sponsoring organization is, among other things, an effective indirect marketing tool. It reinforces that the outplacement firm is conscientious and thorough in carrying out its responsibilities. The importance of servicing the account cannot be overemphasized, as many firms find that their best customers are those who have already purchased outplacement services from them in the past.

There is another major wrinkle to the marketing of outplacement services. Increasingly, there are situations in which the outplacement firm must market itself directly to both the sponsoring organization and the candidate. This is necessary because some sponsoring organizations allow their departing employees, especially at the more senior levels, to "shop" at several different outplacement firms before choosing the one they prefer. The practice of candidate shopping gets some rather mixed reactions. Many outplacement firms disapprove of it. Their rationale is that candidates will find it very confusing to evaluate outplacement firms on solid criteria, especially if they are in a state of heightened emotionality in the aftermath of job loss. Certain sponsoring organizations and candidates, however, welcome the opportunity to shop. They see it as opportunity to exercise some individual control over a very significant career-related decision. Given the increased frequency of this practice, outplacement firms are compelled to attend to the most effective way to market themselves to individual shoppers in addition to corporate sponsors.

Special Considerations

I turn attention now to some of the special challenges that are posed by the marketing of outplacement services. One very important theme concerns the type of interpersonal skills required to be successful at marketing outplacement services. According to Cathcart (1990), to be a successful salesperson one needs skills in three areas—technical, interpersonal, and self-management.

Technical skills refer to product-related knowledge, and the extent to which the marketer truly understands the nature and specifics of the product or service. Interpersonal skills refer to those qualities and behaviors that allow the marketers to apply their technical knowledge in the service of building good relationships with potential buyers. Self-management skills refer to the ability to manage oneself well enough in order to get the job done. The ability to manage time and tension, to complete assignments within deadlines and to maintain an appropriate level of organization are just a few of the important self-management skills.

In most sales situations the emphasis is placed on the technical knowledge skills. The assumption is that the more the marketer knows about the product or service, the more of it they will be able to sell. The technical knowledge skills are seen as more important than the interpersonal or self-management skills. However, in marketing outplacement services the interpersonal and self-management skills far outweigh the technical, because the service itself is not highly technical in nature.

With the possible exception of its office support services, firms are not providing a great deal of technology-based service to outplacement clients. Instead, the service is both intangible and highly personal. The interpersonal skills and job search knowledge of the counselors are paramount. Much of what is being purchased is the knowledge, experience, and judgment of the professional counseling staff. In other words, buyers want to know that the outplacement counselors they have hired have industry knowledge. They also want to be assured that the counselors have the interpersonal and self-management skills to manage successfully emotionally charged and sensitive situations such as job loss.

Buyers look for many of the same qualities and skills in the marketers of outplacement services. They want to be reassured that the marketers, even while promoting their services, have the appropriate level of poise and maturity to handle such sensitive matters. It is not enough to know the product. Rather, the marketers must convince the purchasers that they understand the needs and sensibilities of all the interested parties—the managers who must execute an often difficult decision, the counselors who will eventually assist the candidates, and the candidates themselves whose loss is undeniable and who are likely feeling very vulnerable.

There is another skill that is important for the marketers of outplacement services. It is the ability to work closely with others as a member of an interdependent team. Marketers and counselors rely on one another, and need to coordinate their efforts in relation to the sponsoring organization. Specifically, the marketers are responsible for generating new business. Unless they secure the business, there is no one for the counselors to counsel. However, once the marketer brings in the candidate, the marketer then relies on the counselor to provide excellent service to the candidate. If the quality of the counseling falters, it then becomes much more difficult for the marketer to build further rapport with the sponsoring organization, thereby decreasing the likelihood of repeat business.

There is still another way in which the marketer–counselor relationship is very important. Certain firms utilize a team selling approach where the counselor is actually involved directly in the marketing process. For example, a particular sponsoring organization might want to meet the professional who will be delivering the counseling services before choosing an outplacement firm. Or, they might feel more comfortable receiving their status updates directly from the counselor. In such situations the counselor becomes an integral part of the marketing process. So, because of the interdependent relationship between marketer and counselor, especially in smaller or medium-sized firms, it is very important that the marketer be able to work effectively as a team member.

In summary, the marketing of outplacement services is very much in the tradition of relationship selling. Emphasis is placed on building and maintaining long-term relationships. The marketing can be done by dedicated professionals or by those who also have counseling responsibilities. Marketers strive to distinguish their firms from the competition to gain market share. Outplacement marketers need to be interpersonally skillful. They need maturity, poise, judgment, and trustworthiness to deal with the sensitive issues of job loss.

Chapter 21

Future of Outplacement

The outplacement industry has grown rapidly and impressively since the 1970s. Those in the field have been so busy responding to fast-breaking demands that there has not been much time for evaluating carefully and systematically a whole host of relevant issues. In addition, there are few in the field who are fully trained to conduct behavioral science research. Consequently, although there are many practices that are continued because they appear to work, there are many issues that remain open and deserve more systematic investigation and attention. Hopefully, progress will be made in the years ahead on these issues. R. Lee (1987) divided them into three categories: professional, consulting, and theory and research.

Professional Issues

The first category refers to those issues that are most closely related to the delivery of high-quality counseling services. One major issue concerns the selection, training, and certification of outplacement counselors. As has been indicated several times, outplacement counselors come from a variety of backgrounds. They bring a wide range of skills and styles to the work, and employ an assortment of approaches. Hopefully, in the future, there will be more agreement about what works best for which types of clients under which types of conditions. Some progress has been made in this regard. In the past couple of years the IAOP's Professional Development Committee, under the leadership of Jim Gallagher, has arrived at a set of core competencies for outplacement professionals. The competencies fall into five broad categories: (a) consulting with corporate/organizational clients, (b) consulting with candidates on an individual and/or group basis, (c) assessment, (d) job search training, and (e) career consulting. Although much remains to be done in further refining and operationalizing the specific items within each category, this effort represents an emerging consensus in the field about core competencies. These guidelines can then be used to further refine the training, supervision, and certification of outplacement counselors.

Another issue is the provision of outplacement services for a more heterogeneous group of clients. As the composition of the U.S. workforce becomes increasingly diverse, candidates seen in outplacement will become an even more heterogeneous group than at present. They will vary in age, race, cultural background, employment and educational level, values, goals, and aspirations. This will pose a substantial challenge to outplacement counselors. Practitioners will be called upon to understand even more about the counseling process and the dynamics of building good counselor–client relationships.

In addition, the outplacement industry needs to do a better job of reflecting the diversity of the workforce among its own members. The number of female outplacement consultants has certainly increased in recent years to more accurately reflect the percentage of females in the workforce. However, the percentage of minority counselors remains very small. The profession will need to monitor itself to ensure that it adequately responds to the needs of all its clients.

Another professional issue concerns the proper domain of outplacement counseling, and the extent to which motivational and emotional issues are addressed. A conservative viewpoint would be that outplacement is designed to focus on very specific job search topics and provide concrete assistance around these topics. Emotional support is provided, but it is done only to the extent that it assists the candidate in focusing on concrete job search tasks.

A more liberal stance would be that it is not sufficient to focus only on concrete job search assistance, for many candidates learn all the tips and techniques of job search, but still do not move forward in their searches. For them there are motivational barriers or hurdles that stand in the way. A more broadly defined view of the proper role of outplacement would be that these barriers must be addressed and broken down before the candidate can take advantage of the job search information. Certain of these barriers, such as clinical depression or an anxiety disorder, clearly require referral to a trained mental health professional.

Other situations, however, are not so clear cut. For example, consider the candidate who refuses to initiate networking activity because her or she is very fearful of rejection or because he or she is embarrassed to inform others of the situation. Do outplacement counselors refer such an individual immediately for psychotherapy? Probably not. Yet how far do outplacement counselors go and what methods do they use in addressing these barriers?

The answers are not easily discernible and will vary depending on the problems of the particular client and the skills of the particular counselor. The major point is that the boundaries between career concerns and personal concerns are not always clear cut. Informed judgments must be made. Assisting counselors by establishing more well-defined guidelines is an enormously important counseling challenge that the outplacement field must face.

One of the promising ways in which the outplacement industry might respond to the challenge of assisting individuals in breaking barriers in connection with job search is by making more effective use of job search groups, either alone or, optimally, in combination with individual counseling. Although many outplacement firms have some form of group activity, the groups are not as effective as they might be. Candidates sometimes see the groups as a place where other candidates "moan and groan" and, therefore, find them to be of limited value. Part of the problem could be that the potential benefit of the group is not being fully tapped. A well-led, dynamic job search group in combination with high-quality, individual counseling can produce a potent combination in breaking barriers in connection with candidates' job searches.

Consulting Issues

A second set of issues are those related to the role of outplacement counselors as consultants.

Outplacement counselors, as discussed on several occasions, have a dual allegiance. Counselors are responsible to both the sponsoring organization, who pays for the services, and to the individual candidate who receives them. This dual allegiance can create ethical quandaries from time to time. Decisions about progress reporting, for example, capture the dilemma, especially as it relates to the issue of confidentiality. Typically, outplacement counselors and/or their firm's representative are asked to report to the sponsoring organization concerning client progress. Outplacement counselors must walk the fine line between being responsive to the needs of the sponsoring organization, and being mindful of the sensitivities and trust of the clients who will not want certain personal information to be disclosed. The industry must continue to monitor this and other dilemmas that relate to the dual allegiance. As further experience is accumulated, guidelines must continue to be formulated concerning the appropriate ways for outplacement counselors to respond.

Another consulting issue concerns job development by outplacement firms. There is more than a little irony operating around this issue. In its early days, outplacement practitioners spent considerable time explaining that they were not in the business of finding jobs for candidates, but rather were in the business of providing career planning and job search assistance. Much effort was spent in creating realistic expectations about what outplacement counselors would do for clients and what they would not do. For the most part, it seems that individual candidates came to recognize that, despite their fantasies to the contrary, outplacement firms would not find jobs for them, and that they must accept ultimate responsibility for the outcome of their search. However, in recent years, sponsoring organizations have placed greater pressure on outplacement firms to do more in identifying job openings. Some outplacement firms have also come to see this as a way to gain a competitive edge on their rivals in the marketplace. So, even as the individual outplacement counselor delivers the message to candidates that outplacement, despite its name, is not a placement service, other indicators suggest that the firms will indeed be active in this way. The industry will need to continue to clarify to what extent it will be involved with job lead development. To the extent it is involved in job lead development, it will need to define the boundaries between outplacement firms and recruiting firms.

Another consulting issue concerns the expansion of outplacement services. The use of outplacement services has grown significantly since the 1970s. Most of the largest U.S. corporations provide some form of outplacement services to their employees whose positions have been eliminated. However, even though the growth of industry revenues continues, it has slowed somewhat in the past couple of years, at least in the United States. The industry has suffered diminished profit margins, attributable, in large part, to the increased length of time it takes candidates to find new jobs, as well as the reduced fees charged by outplacement firms. This latter development has been forced by internal industry competition and corporate client "belt tightening" (Franklin, 1991).

Consequently, a number of the largest firms are of the opinion that long-term growth will come from diversifying into other types of human resources consulting. A few of the largest have already developed practices in other areas including organizational planning and development, executive and management assessment, executive coaching, diversity management, and human resources training. Lord (1991) cautioned that entering these areas could put some outplacement firms on the slippery path of competing against much larger, well-established human resources consulting firms. He counseled that outplacement firms build on their expertise carefully, or they could find themselves routed in unfamiliar territory.

There is another area for possible expansion that would seem to build closely on the expertise of outplacement firms—providing career management services to those who have not been terminated by corporations. It is ironic, to say the least, that the very organizations that hire outplacement services to assist terminated employees in getting their work lives back on track, often overlook the trauma of those who remain employed. Those who remain often experience a high level of stress. The stress can be attributable to a number of factors. First, the same amount of work must now be done by fewer workers. Work-related responsibilities might be new or unclear. Those who remain might be experiencing a high degree of guilt or anxiety. "Why did I make it, while others didn't?" "Am I responsible for my friends losing their jobs?" "When is it going to happen to me?" are just some of the lingering questions that might be hanging heavily on the remaining employees. These reactions are part of a phenomenon that is so widespread that it has come to be known as the *survivor syndrome*.

Outplacement counselors have certainly acquired a great deal of firsthand experience in counseling departed employees on issues of career planning and career management. Much of that experience could be used in assisting those still employed on similar issues. In the jargon of outplacement counseling, the skills acquired in working with terminated employees can be *transferred* to working with survivors. As yet, however, corporations seem less willing to provide the same type of assistance to those still on board as has been provided to those displaced. It remains to be seen whether outplacement firms will be successful in expanding to this area.

Theory and Research Issues

The final area of open questions concerns theory and research in the field of outplacement.

According to R. Lee (1987), there is a pressing need for longitudinal studies to measure the long-range effect, if any, of receiving outplacement. It is entirely possible that the outplacement experience has significant value for the candidate in the years following the completion of counseling. There is certainly much anecdotal information to suggest that clients benefit significantly from the experience. The benefits can be around issues of job search, career planning and management, or personal and professional growth. To date, however, there have been no professionally directed studies of these matters.

Certainly, there are formidable challenges involved in conducting quality outcome studies about the effectiveness of using outplacement. Such studies would require two matched groups—one receiving outplacement services, the other receiving no assistance. Also, employees would have to be "matched" in terms of age, experience, personality, and many other factors. Further, the assignment of individuals to a "no-help" group could pose serious ethical problems. Nevertheless, the outplacement industry needs to gather systematically as much information as it can about its effectiveness in order to better understand its practices and strengthen its credibility.

Also, the field of outplacement counseling has the potential to contribute to the development of more sophisticated theories about career development for adults. Broadly speaking, the historical focus of most career development theory has been on young adults, those in the 15- to 25-year-old range. Issues of career selection and entry have dominated. There is a need for theories that concentrate more closely on the career development of older adults. How do adults choose new jobs or careers? Why do some change careers whereas others do not? What factors are important to adults making midlife career decisions? Are these factors different than those of younger adults? How does a termination experience influence future career planning?

There are a whole host of counseling issues to be researched in connection with the delivery of outplacement services. For example, how satisfied are candidates with the outplacement services they receive? What factors contribute to candidate satisfaction? Length of time to complete the search? Salary of new position? Quality of office support services? It is possible that candidate satisfaction has less to do with these factors and much more to do with the quality of the counselor–client relationship. What factors contribute to the formation of a highly satisfying relationship? What qualities or characteristics do successful counselors possess? How can these be measured? How can these be taught?

There are many other questions to be addressed. What is the relation, if any, between successful counseling outcomes and counselor gender, age, sex, educational background? What methods or approaches work best for which type of client? These are just a few of the important relationship issues that deserve more systematic research.

In addition, there are a whole host of issues to be researched at the organizational level. What is the long-range effect on organizational morale and productivity of having to downsize? What factors contribute to an organization's ability to downsize effectively? What type of leadership is most effective during downsizings? What predictions can be made about how various individuals within the organization will respond to downsizings? What is the optimal sequencing and pacing of major downsizings? These are just a few of the organizational issues to be researched.

What becomes apparent is that there are many questions to be researched at several levels of analysis concerning the outplacement process. There are issues that focus on the individual, issues that focus on the counselor–client relationship, and issues that focus on the organization. It is entirely possible that current outplacement practitioners are neither trained nor suited to conduct such research and to generate appropriate theory. If so, links with behavioral scientists could be forged to make possible such inquiry.

Outplacement professionals have developed methods and approaches since the 1970s that they assume to be effective and well-guided. They might be right. In the future, however, the field would, undoubtedly, be strengthened by the systematic collection and analysis of data that can support existing practices or point toward the development of different, more effective ones.

A few final comments are in order concerning the future of outplacement counseling. For most adults, work is a vital part of their life activities. Career-related concerns can, and usually do, have an impact on physical and mental health and on important social relationships. In turn, problems outside the work place influence an individual's performance and satisfaction on the job. It has always been complicated to assist individuals in making sound career-related decisions. With the rapid social and technological changes of the 1990s, meeting the challenge is more complex and important than ever before. As R. Lee (1987) pointed out, as a society we are not in a position to provide guaranteed lifetime employment, but, at the same time, we cannot afford to have skilled and competent workers unemployed for long stretches. Since the 1970s the outplacement industry has come to play a very significant role in assisting people in securing employment and in helping organizations respond to their changing human resources needs. As a result of these important functions, it is an industry that deserves to be more fully understood, judiciously improved, expertly delivered, and wisely used.

Appendix A: Competencies Standards for Outplacement Practitioners as Established by the IAOP, 1992

Category 1: Consulting with corporate/organizational clients, including but not limited to:

- managing corporate relationships
- interpreting business/industry trends and issues
- guiding client organizations and people through transition processes
- preparing managers to handle termination meetings
- managing career centers
- reporting status and results to sponsors
- negotiating reference guidelines and "reason for leaving" statements
- consulting on and providing services dealing with "survivor" issues
- maintaining confidentiality within legal requirements
- working within ethical standards of the profession

Category 2: Consulting with candidates, including but not limited to:

A. On an individual basis
- managing the consultant/candidate relationship
- handling special situations such as "stuck" candidates and candidate dependencies
- problem solving with candidates
- consulting on termination trauma/stress
- motivating candidates through job transition
- identifying candidate "blocks" and referring to other appropriate assistance
- identifying support systems and training candidates to use them effectively
- maintaining confidentiality within legal requirements
- closing the job search and preparing candidates for future assignments
- working within ethical standards of the profession

B. On a group basis
- organizing and administering group programs
- presenting complex data to groups
- maintaining appropriate authority and control
- adapting "individual" issues and procedures (see Category 2A) to groups
- presenting programs on specific subjects related to outplacement (i.e., pre-retirement, survivorship, career transitions, self-employment)

Category 3: Assessment including, but not limited to:

- intake procedures and effectiveness
- analysis/assessment of candidate experiences
- interpreting and/or reporting and applying results of standardized measurements
- identifying critical skills and accomplishments
- identifying values that apply to work

Category 4: Job search training, including but not limited to:

- strategy and planning job campaigns
- research methods
- networking and other search techniques
- developing resumes and other campaign tools
- developing interviewing skills and protocols
- teaching salary negotiations
- evaluating/negotiating job offers
- understanding business/economic trends
- developing job opportunities
- utilizing other resources for support/assistance
- job market data interpretation
- developing/utilizing specific employer data

Category 5: Career consulting, including but not limited to:

- developing individual specific career plans with defined goals
- life/work planning
- career change/options consulting
- career decision making
- identifying personal/environmental issues that impact career decisions
- identifying/exploring self-employment options
- mastery/use of career resource information
- interpreting corporate cultures and structures
- developing educational plans to support career goals

Appendix B: Standards of Ethical Practice for Outplacement Professionals Established by the IAOP, 1993

Definition of Terms

IAOP refers to the International Association of Outplacement Professionals
The association refers to the International Association of Outplacement Professionals
Consultant refers to any outplacement consultant
Corporate client refers to the corporation requesting and paying for the outplacement work
Candidate refers to persons receiving consulting service

Preamble

Outplacement consultants must maintain the highest level of professional conduct with both corporate clients and candidates. Outplacement consultants are responsible for continuing their professional growth throughout their career, including knowledge of Standards for Ethical Practice. In the outplacement consulting relationship, the consultant should maintain respect for the candidate and focus the outplacement activities towards a positive resolution for the candidate. While marketing services, outplacement consultants should neither claim nor imply professional qualifications exceeding those possessed. Outplacement consultants must recognize their boundaries of competence and provide only those services and use only those techniques for which they are qualified by training or experience. When outplacement consultants are providing case information to the public or client organizations, they need to ensure that the content is general, unidentifiable candidate information which is accurate, unbiased, and consists of objective, factual data.

136

Standards

Each member will abide by the association's Standards for Ethical Practice in all professional activities to move toward a positive resolution of the outplacement process for both the candidate and corporate client.

All outplacement professionals shall:

- Continuously improve their professional skills, competency and knowledge to provide the highest level of service to organizations and those counseled;
- Maintain the confidentiality of the relationship between consultant and candidate;
- Conduct themselves according to the following values: concern and respect for others, development of an individual's self-esteem, dignity of the individual, honesty and integrity;
- Encourage and assist the candidate to take responsibility for decisions during the employment transition;
- Comply with all laws, statutes, and regulations affecting business practices and relations with corporate clients and candidates;
- Provide full disclosure of any potential conflicts of interest in the course of their professional practice;
- Refrain from using their position, influence, or knowledge to secure special gain for themselves or their business;
- Clearly define the deliverables to both the candidate and the corporate clients, and ensure these commitments are within their knowledge and abilities, and are met;
- Practice respect for the individual without regard to race, ancestry, place of origin, religion, ethnic origin, citizenship, creed, gender, sexual orientation, disability, age, or marital status.

Consulting Relationship With Corporations

Consulting refers to the relationship between a professional helper and help-needing individual, group or client organization in which the consultant is providing assistance in defining and solving a work-related problem or potential problem.

1. A consultant must have a high degree of awareness of his or her own values, knowledge, skills, limitations, and needs in entering a consulting relationship.
2. The consultant must establish understanding and agreement with the corporate client for the problem definition, goals, and results.

3. The consultant is responsible to ensure that he or she or the organization represented has the necessary competencies and resources for giving the corporate client the kind of help that is needed. Appropriate referral resources should be available.
4. The consulting relationship should encourage corporate client growth toward self-direction. The consultant must maintain this role consistently and not become a decision maker for the corporate client or create a future dependency on the consultant.
5. Consultants shall not knowingly accept a corporate consulting assignment where it is impossible or unlikely that they can make a positive impact.
6. Consultants shall have formal and effective means for ensuring professional quality and integrity of services they provide. These means may include, but need not be confined to, internal review by supervisors or peers, and surveys of candidate satisfaction during and after the provision of outplacement consulting.

Consulting Relationship With Candidates

This section refers to practice issues of individual and/or group consulting relationships.

1. The consultant's obligation is to respect the integrity and promote the welfare of the candidate, whether the candidate is assisted individually or in a group relationship.
2. Subject to applicable legal constraints, consultants must make provisions for maintaining confidentiality in the creation, storage and disposal of records. The consulting relationship and information resulting therefrom must be kept confidential, unless with the candidate's written consent.
3. Private information can be disclosed to others only with the informed written consent of the candidate, or as legally required.
4. When the candidate's condition indicates that there is a clear and imminent danger to the candidate or others, the consultant must take reasonable action or inform responsible authorities, ideally with the candidate's knowledge or permission, but if necessary without. Consultation with psychologists, psychiatrists, and legal authorities should be used if a serious threat exists.
5. The consultant must inform the candidate and corporate client of the purposes, goals, techniques, rules of procedures and limitations that may affect the relationship at or before the time that the outplacement consulting relationship is entered.
6. If the consultant determines his or her inability to be of professional assistance to the candidate, the consultant must either avoid initiating the outplacement consulting relationship or immediately terminate the relationship. In either event, the consultant must suggest appropriate alternatives.
7. The consultant must ensure that the relationship with any candidate remains professional at all times.

8. The consulting relationship should encourage candidate growth toward self-direction. The consultant must maintain this role consistently and not become a decision maker for the candidate or create a future dependency on the consultant.

Assessment

The primary purpose of assessment if to provide descriptive measures that are objective and interpretable in either comparative or absolute terms. The consultant must interpret the statements that follow as applying to the whole range of appraisal techniques including tests and nontest data. Test results constitute only one of a variety of pertinent sources of information for career planning and counseling decisions. Consulting with suitably trained consultants is required when the outplacement consultant lacks expertise in this area.

1. Different tests demand different levels of competence for administration, scoring and interpretation. Consultants must recognize the limits of their competence and perform only those functions for which they are licensed, certified, or educationally prepared. The consultant must provide specific directions and/or feedback to the examinee prior to and following the test administration. The purpose of testing and the explicit use of the tests must be known to the examinee prior to testing. The consultant is responsible for interpreting test results and must have the qualifications and understanding of educational and psychological measurement, validation criteria, and test research.
2. In selecting tests for use in a given situation with a particular candidate, the consultant must consider carefully the specific validity, reliability, and appropriateness of the test(s).
3. In situations where a computer is used for test administration and scoring, the consultant is responsible for ensuring that the administration and scoring program functions properly to provide accurate test results.
4. Tests must be administered under the same conditions that were established in their standardization. Unsupervised or inadequately supervised test-taking, such as the use of tests through the mail, is considered unethical. (Unless the test publisher permits unsupervised test-taking.)
5. The meaningfulness of test results used in career planning and counseling functions generally depends on the examinee's unfamiliarity with specific items of the test. Any prior coaching or dissemination of test materials can invalidate test results. Therefore, test security is one of the professional obligations of consultants.
6. The examinee's welfare and prior explicit understanding must be a criterion for determining the recipients of the test results. The consultant must see that specific interpretation accompanies any release of individual or group test data. The interpretation of test data must be related to the examinee's particular concerns.

7. Consultants must be cautious when interpreting the results of research instruments that are based on insufficient technical data.

8. The outplacement consultant must proceed with caution when attempting to evaluate and interpret the performance of minority group members or other persons who are not represented in the norm group on which the instrument was standardized.

9. Consultants must recognize when test results have become obsolete. The consultant will avoid and prevent the misuse of obsolete test results.

10. The consultant must guard against the appropriation, reproduction, or modification of published tests or parts thereof, without acknowledgement and permission from the publisher.

11. Regarding the preparation, publication, and distribution of tests, reference in the United States should be made to:
    a. "Standards for Educational and Psychological Tests," revised edition, 1985, published by the American Psychological Association on behalf of itself, the Educational Research Association, and the National Council of Measurement and Education.
    b. "The Responsible Use of Tests: A Position Paper of AMEG, APGA, and NCME," *Measurement and Evaluation in Guidance,* 1972, 5, 385-388.
    c. "Responsibilities of Users of Standardized Tests," APGA, *Guidepost,* October 5, 1989, pp. 5-8.

*Countries outside the United States should utilize like references in their country to determine ethical use of assessment instruments.

Conduct of Outplacement Professional Practices

1. In advertising or marketing services, a consultant must present services in a manner that accurately informs what professional services are available.

2. Consultants must present their affiliation with any organization accurately in terms of sponsorships or certification by that organization.

3. A consultant has an obligation to withdraw from a consulting relationship if it is believed that the relationship will result in violation of the ethical standards.

4. An outplacement consultant shall not invest in or utilize business ideas or plans developed by candidates.

5. Outplacement consultants will not accept outplacement and search or placement fees for the same candidate.

Business Development Practices

1. Advertising by members shall be factual, dignified and otherwise consistent with the purpose of the profession.
2. An outplacement professional will not agree to pay employees of sponsoring organizations for referrals, or offer rebates, allowances, or gifts to sponsored candidates.
3. In marketing or advertising outplacement services, an outplacement professional shall not speak or write derogatory comments about other outplacement professionals and/or firms.
4. Outplacement consultants must not misrepresent services offered corporate clients and/or candidates.

Appendix C:Resources for Outplacement Practitioners

Selected Sources of Business Information

Reference Books to Identify Sources of Information

- Business Information Desk Reference
- Directories in Print
- Encyclopedia of Associations
- Encyclopedia of Business Information Sources
- Getting the "Low-Down" on Employers and a "Leg-Up" on the Job Market
- How to Find Information About Companies
- Professional Careers Sourcebook
- Researching Your Way to a Good Job
- The Encyclopedia of Managerial Job Descriptions

Corporate Information—General Sources

- Directory of Corporate Affiliations
- Directory of Leading Private Companies
- Dun & Bradstreet Directory of Service Companies
- Dun & Bradstreet Million Dollar Directory
- Dun & Bradstreet Regional Business Directories
- International Directory of Corporate Affiliations
- Macrae's Blue Book
- Moody's Manuals
- Over-The-Counter 1,000 Yellow Book
- Standard Industrial Classification (SIC) Manual
- Standard & Poor's Corporation Records
- Standard & Poor's Register of Corporations, Directors, and Executives
- State Industrial Directories

- Thomas' Register of American Manufacturers
- Ward's Business Directory of U.S. Private and Public Companies
- Ward's Directory of 49,000 Private and Public Companies

Corporate Information—Specialized Sources

- Consultants and Consulting Organizations Directory
- Corp Tech's Directory of Small High-Tech Companies
- Directory of American Firms Operating in Foreign Countries
- Directory of Foreign Firms Operating in the U.S.
- Dun's Consultants Directory
- O'Dwyer's Directory of Corporate Communications
- O'Dwyer's Directory of Public Relations Firms
- Polk's World Bank Directory
- Pratt's Guide to Venture Capital Sources
- Standard Directory of Advertisers
- Standard Directory of Advertising Agencies

Industry Surveys

- Fortune Double 500
- Standard & Poor's Industry Surveys
- U.S. Industrial Outlook

Periodicals/Journals

- Barron's
- Business Week
- Forbes
- Fortune
- Harvard Business Review
- Industry Week
- Inc
- National Business Employment Weekly
- The New York Times
- Occupational Outlook Quarterly
- The Wall Street Journal

Indexes to Business Periodicals

- ABI/Inform
- Business Periodicals Index
- Guide to Special Issues and Indexes of Periodicals
- New York Times Index

- Predicast's Funk & Scott Index of Corporations and Industries
- Wall Street Journal Index

CD-ROM and Other Computer-Based Sources

- ABI/Inform Ondisc (CD-ROM)
- Business Periodicals Ondisc (CD-ROM)
- Business Periodicals Index (CD-ROM)
- Corporate and Industry Research Reports (CD-ROM)
- Dun's Million Dollar Disc (CD-ROM)
- F & S Plus Text (CD-ROM)
- Infotrac (laser disc)
- Laser Disclosure (CD-ROM)
- Moody's Company Data (CD-ROM)
- Nexis Library (on-line service)
- Standard & Poor's Corporations (CD-ROM)
- Thomas' Register (CD-ROM)
- The Wall Street Journal (CD-ROM)

Overview of Career Planning/Job Search

- *Guerrilla Tactics in the Job Market,* Tom Jackson
- *How to Seek a New and Better Job,* William Gerraughty
- *The Complete Job-Search Handbook,* Howard Figler
- *Through the Brick Wall,* Kate Wendleton
- *What Color is Your Parachute?,* Richard Bolles

Advice on Career Management

- *Careering and Re-Careering for the 1990's,* Ronald Krannich
- *Conduct Expected,* William Lareau
- *Shifting Gears,* Carole Hyatt
- *Smart Moves,* Godfrey Golzen & Andrew Garner
- *Staying Employed,* Tom Daoust
- *What Your Boss Can't Tell You,* Kent Straat

References

Amundson, N.E., & Borgen, W.A. (1987). Coping with unemployment: What helps and what hinders. *Journal of Employment Counseling, 24,* 97–106.

Amundson, N.E., & Borgen, W.A. (1988). Factors that help and hinder in group employment counseling. *Journal of Employment Counseling, 25,* 104–114.

The Association of Outplacement Consulting Firms. (1991, October). *Casebook on Ethics and Standards For the Practice of Corporate Outplacement.* Washington, DC: Author.

Axmith, M. (1991). The ethics of outplacement. *Career Planning and Adult Development Journal, 7*(3), 6–10.

Backover, A. (1991, April 18). Cultural barriers impede job search. American Counseling Association. *Guidepost,* p.1.

Bolles, R.N. (1994). *What color is your parachute?* Berkeley, CA: Ten Speed Press.

Bordin, E.S. (1975). The generalizability of the psychoanalytic concept of the working alliance. *Psychotherapy: Theory, Research, and Practice, 16,* 252–260.

Bowers, S., & Pickman, A. (1991, October). *The counselor–candidate relationship in outplacement.* Paper presented to the Association of Outplacement Consulting Firms, Chicago, IL.

Bowers, S., & Pickman, A. (1993, May). *Counselor burnout: What is it?* Paper presented to the International Association of Outplacement Professionals, New York.

Brickman, P., Rabinowitz, V.C., Karuza, J., Coates, D., Cohn, E., & Kidder, L. (1982). Models of helping and coping. *American Psychologist, 37,* 368–384.

Bridges, W. (1988). *Surviving corporate transition.* New York: Doubleday.

Brittain, W.P. (1982). Outplacement visited: The new old personnel function. In R.M. O'Brien, A.M. Dickinson, & M.P. Rosow (Eds.), *Industrial behavior modification* (pp. 286–297). New York: Pergamon Press.

Byrd, V. (1993, March 7). The struggle for minority managers. *New York Times,* p. 27.

Cathcart, J. (1990). *Relationship selling.* New York: Perigee Books.

Consult America. (1989). *Outplacement consulting in the United States in 1989—Issues, marketing and trends.* Concord, MA: Author.

Coopers & Lybrand. (1991). *Severance pay policies and practices.* New York: Author.

Dumas, L.S. (1992, March/April). Daddy got fired ... are we going to be poor? *Psychology Today,* pp. 30–33.

Edelwich, J., & Brodsky, A. (1980). *Burnout: Stages of disillusionment in the helping profession.* New York: Human Sciences Press.

Ellis, A. (1984). Rational-emotive therapy. In R. J. Corsini (Ed.), *Current psychotherapies* (3rd ed., pp. 196–238). Itasca, IL: Peacock.

Epstein, L., & Feiner, A.H. (1988). Countertransference: The therapist's contribution to treatment. In B. Wolstein (Ed.), *Essential papers on countertransference* (pp. 282–303). New York: New York University Press.

Figler, H. (1988). *The complete job search handbook.* New York: Henry Holt.

Franklin, S. (1991, October 20). The squeeze on outplacement firms. *Chicago Tribune,* p. B3.

Freeman, S.C., & Haring-Hidore, M. (1988). Outplacement for underserved women workers. *Journal of Career Development, 14*(4), 287–293.

Freudenberger, H., & Richelson, G. (1980). *Burnout: The melancholia of high achievement.* New York: Anchor Press, Doubleday.

Gallagher, J.J. (1982). *What makes a good career consultant?* New York: Author.

Gallagher, J.J. (1990). *A baseline survey, practitioners of outplacement.* New York: Author.

Garfield, S.L. (1989). *The practice of brief psychotherapy.* New York: Pergamon Press.

Gelso, C.J., & Carter, J.A. (1985). The relationship in counseling and psychotherapy: Components, consequences, and theoretical antecedents. *The Counseling Psychologist, 13*, 155–243.

Hansen, J.I.C., & Campbell, D.P. (1985). *Manual for the Strong Interest Inventory.* Palo Alto, CA: Consulting Psychologists Press.

Harding, C.F. (1991, September 15). Uniting your family during a job search. *National Business Employment Weekly*, pp. 9–10.

Harrison, S. (1992). IRS: Outplacement services are not gross income. *The IAOP Networks, 2*(3), 1.

Holland, J.L. (1973). *Making vocational choices: A theory of careers.* Englewood Cliffs, NJ: Prentice-Hall.

Holmes, T.H., & Rahe, R.H. (1967). Social readjustment rating scale. *Journal of Psychosomatic Research, 11,* 213–218.

Industry overviews. (1993, April 19). *Fortune*, p. 254.

Jones, J. (1981). Diagnosing and treating staff burnout among health professionals. In J.W. Jones (Ed.), *The burnout syndrome* (pp. 107–126). Park Ridge, IL: London House Management Press.

Jung, C.G. (1971). *Psychological types.* Palo Alto, CA: Consulting Psychologists Press.

Kubler-Ross, E. (1975). *Death: The final stage of growth.* Englewood Cliffs, NJ: Prentice-Hall.

Lee, C.C., & Richardson, B.L. (1991). Promise and pitfalls of multicultural counseling. In C.C. Lee & B.L. Richardson (Eds.), *Multicultural issues in counseling* (pp. 3–9). Alexandria, VA: American Association for Counseling and Development.

Lee, M.A. (1990). Managing up for a successful corporate career—Especially if you're Asian-American. *Uptrend, 4*(2), 1.

Lee, R.J. (1987). *Outplacement counseling for the terminated manager.* New York: Lee Hecht Harrison.

Le Hane, L.J. (1990). AOCF: An 8-year old, meeting significant challenges. In *The directory of outplacement firms, 1990–91* (p. 41). Fitzwilliam, NH: Kennedy Publications.

Leibowitz, Z.B., Farren, C., & Kaye, B.L. (1986). *Designing career development systems.* San Francisco, CA: Jossey-Bass.

Lord, D.A. (1991, November). Outplacement's agony: Just growing pains? *Executive Recruiter News*, p. 2.

Maslach, C., & Solomon, T. (1980). *Pressures toward dehumanization from within and without.* Unpublished paper, University of California at Berkeley.

Mejías, C. (1993, May). *International issues in outplacement.* Paper presented to the International Association of Outplacement Professionals, New York.

Milligan, M.V. (1992). What does it take to be an effective outplacement counselor? In *The directory of outplacement firms, 1993–94* (pp. 47–50). Fitzwilliam, NH: Kennedy Publications.

Morin, W.J., & Yorks, L. (1990). *Dismissal.* New York: Drake Beam Morin.

Murray, C. (1993, May). *Outplacement in Europe.* Paper presented to the International Association of Outplacement Professionals, New York.

Myers, I.B., & McCaulley, M.H. (1985). *Manual: A guide to the development and use of the Myers–Briggs Type Indicator.* Palo Alto, CA: Consulting Psychologists Press.

National Career Development Association. (1990). *National survey of working America, 1990.* Alexandria, VA: Author.

O'Leary, K.D., & Wilson, G.T. (1975). *Behavior therapy: Application and outcome.* Englewood Cliffs, NJ: Prentice-Hall.

Paine, W.S. (1981). The burnout syndrome in context. In J.W. Jones (Ed.), *The burnout syndrome* (pp. 1–29). Park Ridge, IL: London House Management Press.

Phelps, S., & Mason, M. (1991, August). When women lose their jobs. *Personnel Journal,* pp. 64–68.

Prichard, P. (1992, June). *Outplacement/career counseling: A new paradigm? The advantage of groups.* Paper presented to the Career Development Specialists Network (CDSN), New York.

Report of the Research Task Force of the National Institute of Mental Health. (1975). *Research in the service of mental health* (DHEW Publication No. (ADM) 75–236). Rockville, MD: NIMH.

Stoltenberg, C.D., & Delworth, U. (1988). *Supervising counselors and therapists.* San Francisco, CA: Jossey-Bass.

Sweet, D.H. (1989). *A manager's guide to conducting terminations.* Lexington, MA: Lexington Books.

Sywak, M. (1992). The career development professional. In D.H. Montross & C.J. Shinkman (Eds.), *Career development: Theory and practice* (pp. 293–305). Springfield, IL: Charles Thomas.

Wakelee-Lynch, J. (1989, December 28). Cincinnati clips. American Counseling Association. *Guidepost,* p. 10.

Wendleton, K. (1992). *Through the brick wall.* New York: Villard Books.

Williams, L. (1992, December 15). Companies capitalizing on worker diversity. *New York Times,* p. A1.

Wolpe, J. (1969). *The practice of behavior therapy.* New York: Pergamon.

Index

Printed in the United States
by Baker & Taylor Publisher Services